Systematic Description of Fruit Crops

KANCHAN K. SRIVASTAVA

M.Sc. (Ag), Ph.D.
Professor Horticulture (IAS, BHU), Assistant (SS),
Division of Pomology,
Sher-e-Kashmir University of Agricultural Sciences and Technology of Kashmir, Shalimar, Srinagar,
Jammu and Kashmir -191 121

International Book Distributing Co.
(Publishing Division)

Published by
INTERNATIONAL BOOK DISTRIBUTING CO.
(Publishing Division)
Khushnuma Complex Basement
7, Meerabai Marg (Behind Jawahar Bhawan)
Lucknow 226 001 U.P. (INDIA)
Tel. : 91-522-2209542, 2209543, 2209544, 2209545
Fax : 0522-4045308
E-Mail : ibdco@airtelmail.in

First Edition 2009

ISBN 81-8189-272-0

Composed & Designed at :

Panacea Computers
3rd Floor, Agarwal Sabha Bhawan, Subhash Mohal
Sadar Cantt. Lucknow-226 002
Tel : 0522-2483312, 9335927082
E-mail : prasgupt@rediffmail.com

Printed at:

Salasar Imaging Systems
C-7/5, Lawrence Road Industrial Area
Delhi - 110 035
Tel. : 011-27185653, 9810064311

Dedicated to
My Beloved Mother
Smt. Prema Devi

Prof. Anwar Alam
Vice-Chancellor

Sher-e-Kashmir
University of Agricultural Sciences
& Technology of Kashmir

FOREWORD

With the advent of World Trade Organization regime, lot of advancement has taken place in the Agricultural Education. The exercise has been done to revise PG curricula and syllabi for the masters' degree programmes. The mission of the agricultural education is excellence in related science and techonology, increasing production, productivity and profitability for livelihood security at the same time sustainability. It is need of the hour to adopt utilitarian approach aiming at producing professionals and academicians who are self reliant, self confident and self competing individuals. Indian Council of Agricultural Research, New Delhi has implemented uniform syllabi in Agricultural education ensuring converge to certain essential subject matter.

'Systematic Pomology' is basic course taught in the Masters programme. It deals with various kind of fruit plants, scientific description, nomenclature, classification on the basis of morphology, genetics, anatomy and biochemistry. Except some basic botany and taxonomy no book wholly cover systematic descriptin of fruits crops. A need for such a book was being felt by academician for some time.

I am happy that the present book "**Systematic Description of Fruit Crops**" has been prepared which bridges gap and will be useful to academicians and researchers alike. It is very comprehensive covering all important temperate, tropical and subtropical fruit crops. I congratulate Dr. K.K. Srivastava for his endeavor bringing out this book for aspirants.

(Anwar Alam)

PREFACE

Systematic Pomology is basic course for the post graduate students taught all over India. Though understanding of the systematic position of the fruit crops are imperative not only for the students but all those who are involved for the development of the horticulture especially Plant breeder, Geneticist, Cytologist, Botanist, Chemist, Entomologist, Plant Pathologist, Taxonomist and Paleo-Botanist. There are Large number of books available in the Library related to Botany covering partially various topics of the fruit botany. But none book enables to satisfy the need of the researcher, post graduate and under graduate students, though it is basic and core course in the Indian Council of Agricultural Research curriculum. Viewing the above fact, this book has been prepared to cater the long felt needs of the undergraduate, post graduate students and researchers and teachers. Effort has been made to make such a book to the level that it might be used as basic book for needy. The author is continuously teaching the systematic course for the last seven years which inspired the author for the preparation of the manuscript.

Author acknowledge sincere thanks and gratitude to all those whose books, popular articles, research papers, review papers has been consulted during the course of preparation of the manuscript.

Thanks are also acknowledged to Hon'ble Vice Chancellor Prof Anwar Alam, Director Research Dr A.R. Trag, and Head Division of Pomology SKUAST(K) and for providing friendly atmosphere to move ahead in this direction. My sincere thanks to Prof R.K. Pathak, Ex- Director, Central Institue for Sub-Tropical Horticulture and Late Prof Ç.B.S. Rajput, Ex-Director, IAS, BHU who has always been an inspiring icon for the Horticulturist. I have to thanks to my senior colleague Prof. F.A. Banday, Dr M. Feza Ahmed (Senior Scientist), Dr M.K. Sharma, Dr S.R. Singh, Mr. Amarjeet Singh (Assistant Professors) for moral and technical support.

I bow my head with sincere gratitude for my Father who is showering the choicest blessings from the heaven. My mother Smt. Prema Devi with whom I learned the first lesson. I wish to thanks my elder brother Mr Satish Kumar, Smt. Kamla Devi, Mr. Krishna Kumar Srivastava, Neelesh, Smt. Leena, Mr Amitabh Pooja Nigam, Mr Anupam Srichandra, without their love and blessings it was impossible to take the task.

I can't underline my better half Ms. Shalu Srivastava and my baby boy Master Lakshya who's inspiring gesture given me strength to prepare the manuscript in such rigorous bone shaking cold.

Lastly, I very sincerely hope that the students, teachers and researchers will find this book to be beneficial for them. I shall be thankful to your friendly suggestions and corrections in subsequent edition.

Place: Srinagar **Dr. Kanchan K. Srivastava**

Contents

Chapter 1

Introduction and Importance of Systematic Description

India endowed with a wide range of agro-climatic conditions, enjoys enviable positions in the horticultural map of world. Almost all type of fruit crops are grown. Horticulture occupies 6.7% of gross cropped area of the country. Horticulture contributes 18% of gross value of agricultural output and 52% of export earnings in agriculture. As a result, horticulture today is not merely a means of diversification but form an integral part of food and nutritional security as also an essential ingredient of economic security. India is an important hub of natural diversity. Vavilov, developed geographic centre of variability. He identified Asia as a major centre with Indian Centre of N.E. region as primary or secondary centre of origin for many crop plants. A wider genetic base assumes priority in plant breeding research aimed at developing new varieties for increased crop production. Crop improvement programme based on wider genetic base and hybridization knowledge of systematic description of fruit crops are quite imperative, in other word, systematic pomology is a backbone of plant science. The subject Pomology integrates specialized knowledge from field of geography, metrology, climatology, soil science, chemistry, physics, nutrition, genetics, fruit breeding, pathology, entomology, economics, business and resource management.

Systematic pomology deals with the scientific grouping of the fruit plants taking consideration of anatomical, morphological, physiological, genetical and environmental characteristics.

Importance

i. Systematic description helps in naming identification and grouping of plants.

ii. It is essential for crop breeder.

iii. It is helpful to mycologist and cytologist.

iv. It helps in selection of crop varieties resistant to insect pest and disease.

v. Helps in direct selection of variety for cultivation.

vi. Knowledge of systematic description of crops are essential for exchange of idea for correspondence, because of fact few lac species are existing in world ranging from *Sequa zegansia*_having height 278 feet, 37 feet dia to bacteria having 1/50 thousand micron long from strawberry, cape goase berry, passion fruit to mango, Jamun, Jackfruit, Walnut, hence, some kind of ordering, grouping is imperative necessary for ease in identification and study. It is generally believed that as many as 500 myriad of species of plants, animals and micro-organisms inhabited this earth since life began over 3.5 billions years age, many of them have disappeared during the normal evolutionary course, some having left their descendants and surviving remnants. At present, glaring discrepancy exists on data pertaining to actual number of species on the earth, the figure varies from 5-100 million. WCM (1992) suggests a conservative estimate of 12.5 million. However, surprisingly today 1.4 million species have been identified and described and over million still remain unclassified. Total estimated number of plants species in the world are 4.80 lakhs (out of 3,2 2311 (67%) species have been identified.

The term systematic is scientific study of inter relationship, taxonomy, identification, nomenclature and their classification into different groups according to their morphological, physiological and reproductive resemblance. So for as angiosperms or higher plants are concerned over 1, 99,000 species (1,59,000 dicotyledons and 40,000 monocotyledons) are already known to us and much more are being unveiled. Plants are not numerous but varied in habit and habitat. Over 3,00,000 species of plants when looked upon within this perspective have remained a question and puzzle for taxonomist. The principle objective of systematic description of various fruit crops are to distinguish plants in various groups and clarify plants in such a manner that their relationship with regard to their descent from a common ancestry may be easily brought out. Classification is to arrange plants in such a manner to get an idea for the sequence of their evolution from simpler, easier to more complex, more recent and more advanced type.

The taxonomy term was coined by A.P. De Condole (1813) in his *Theorie Etementaire de la botanique* and is a part of systematic concerned for the study of principles, procedure, rules, regulations and basis of classification. The term systematic and taxonomy are synonyms. In taxonomic study, the group of any rank is termed as taxon (Taxa-plural). Taxonomy is an oldest branch of plant science, was briefly started as science of briefs morphological description, especially reproductive parts. Further, with the advancement in technology especially highly magnifying microscopes, was an example, which could advance the knowledge by more details of anatomy and cytology. In recent past development of polymerase chain reaction (PCR machine) and analysis of plant cell composition opens new avenues of plant taxonomic study. Morphological characters, chemical composition and cytological information was in practice from long for the classification of fruit plants. However, these techniques possess certain limitations as they could be influenced by environmental and development effects. The advanced technique like molecular markers are now more precisely being employed for plant classification and breeding. In molecular markers enzyme based isozyme patterns, in which different forms as an enzyme exhibiting the same catalytic activity but differing in charge and electroheretic mobility. The enzyme of interest can be detected by treating the gel (polyacrylamidgel) with specific activity strains. The different banding pattern are obtained in isozyme analysis, such variation can be used for sorting out characters of interest. DNA based molecular markers found most suitable techniques for identification of individual as it is more stable. Restriction Fragment Length Polymorphism (RFLP), Amplified Fragment Length Polymorphism (AFLP), Single-Strand Conformation Polymorphism (SSC), Sequence Characterized Amplified Regions (SCAR), Single Primer Amplification Reaction (SPAR), Sequenced Tagged Sites (STS) and Cleaved Amplified Polymorphism (CAP) are important DNA based molecular markers. Polymorphism in nucleotide sequence is function as molecular marker in mapping.

The widely accepted and only one taxonomic structure is mainly based on the morphological principles. Recent past recommendations have also been made to introduce palynological, cytological, anatomical, biochemical, physiological and cytogenetical evidences in addition to palaeobotanical evidences for determination of any taxon. Numerical taxonomy is practiced to establish classification in the case date obtained from various botanical characters are a tabulated and analyzed more conveniently with the help of computers and numerical methods. Numerical taxonomist do the grouping of taxonomic units by numerical methods.

There are millions of plants showing similarities as well as differences at none of them are identical. The fundamental idea of the plants is pre-requisite for systematic classification. The study of systematic is linked with other branches of science helps in building up of taxonomy.

The systematized study has benefited not only botanist or systematic scientist but all those who concerned with forestry, plant breeding and genetics, coal, paper industry, and food as such this helps in order to procurement of proper materials for crop improvement programme. Taxonomy are closely related thus without its knowledge it is impossible to identify and compare plants for execution of hybridization programme. Environment has significant role in plant sciences, it affect plant ideotype. *Agriculture and horticulture have direct bearing on taxonomy.* Taxonomy has great importance for fossil identification as such its identification is possible only when adequate literature on the living plants are available. The knowledge regarding living plants and their literature helps to establish linkage amongst taxa.

Systematics

Systematics may be defined as scientific domain. Which deals with type and diversity of biological organism and any or all relationships amongest them. It is not only grouping and naming of organism but, basic feature of each texa, its correlation with other and their evolution.

Taxonomy

According to Simpson (1961) as the study of classification, its procedure, rules, basis and principles.

Classification

Classification is the orderly arrangement of organism into groups or categories based on their relationship. The term relationship indicates the morphological, historical, cytological, cytogenetical, biochemical data, AFLP,RFLP and DNA finger printing techniques.

Chapter **2**

System and Principle of Classification

Importance of plants for human being is well known its close link with tedious of plant identification and isolation of plants especially for commercial use. Plant classification was seriously attempted after sixteenth century. Theophrastus (9370-285 BC) and Dioscorides (1st century A.D.) were earliest workers in classification system when botanical knowledge has scarcely advanced. Linnaeus formulated certain principles of plant taxonomy in his book *Critica Botanica,* further John Lindley, Adanson de Candolle and Sir Joseph, Hooker followed Linnaeus. However, the concept did not received much attention adopt choice of wide range of development of numerical taxonomy led to characters for classification. Theophrastus, hence known father of Botany. The plants were studied and grouped mostly from utilitarian point of view. Old system of classification were more or less artificial, plants being classified on the basis of one or few characters. The very early system of plant classification is depicted in Lindley's "*Vegetable Kingdom*" published in 1846 and Rendle's *classification of Flowering plants,* vol I, published in 1904. the other important work in the area of systematic description of plants which received much attention are the *Genera Plantarium* by Bentham and Hooker descriptive period of classification started from the period of Tournefort, Jussieu Brown, John Lindley, G.Bentham, Endmund Bossier, Curt Von Sprengel, Edward V Regal and Asa Grey. Their works are principally concerned with flower description published in 1862-83 and (2) *"Die naturlichen pflanzenfamilien"* of Engler and Prantl, published in 1887-1909. The *Genera Plantarum* of Bentham and Hooker is the elaboration of de Candolle system. But from phylogenetic point of view both the systems are not very satisfactory. John Hutchinson (1926, 1934, 1959 and 1973) made the most recent and widely accepted attempt to classify flowering plants on the basis of phylogenetic base. With the advancement of research, knowledge and technology it has became more evident that chromosome characters, biochemical ecological and palynological investigations have greatly influenced the plant classification more précised. The genetical constituents and biochemical, correlations between plants are of major significance. Modern scientific informations are being more precisely used for evolution classification rather than descriptive taxonomy. Morphological features do have their own significance particularly as an aid to identification and they have been more convenient for primary delimitation of texa.

Bailey (1949) has said if a truly natural classification of plants is to be attained, it must comprise on the analysis and harmonization of evidence from all organs and parts. The objective of modern taxonomy must satisfy aforementioned points 1) to provide a convenient method of identification 2) to establish natural relationship 3) to detect evolution of work, discovery its processes and interpreting its result.

Criteria for Determination of Taxonomy

The morphological characters of plants are still significant method for identification and classification of plants are based on the principle of morphological feature. Their reproductive and vegetative features are taken into consideration the vegetative characters viz. type of the root, nature of stem, its appearance, branching habit, texture, growth pattern, leaf arrangement, to size and venation are studied for vegetative characters. In reproductive characters floral part arrangements and their number, shape and pattern of growth. Sometimes plants show resemblances in floral characters but differ in vegetative features vice-versa because all parts of plants may not be necessarily evolve at similar time and hence, these differences constitute the criteria for taxonomic purpose. Besseyan (1915) suggested following points as criteria for plant classification.

i) Living beings have advanced from simple to complex form.

ii) Evolutionary transformations are irreversible and permanent.

iii) Existing simple forms are like their ancestors than existing complex form.

iv) The herbaceous habit is more advanced in comparison to woody similarly annuals are more advanced than biennials.

v) In angiosperm simple leaves are more primitive than compound leaves.

vi) Monoecisms are more primitive than dioecism.

vii) Solitary flowers are more primitive than aggregated.

viii) Actinomorphic flowers are more primitive than zygomorphic.

ix) Hypogynous, apocarpous, are more primitive than perigynous and epigynous and syncarpus pistil.

x) Free stamens are more primitive than adelphous stamens.

xi) Similarly simple fruits are more primitive than compound.

Anatomical criteria is also important consideration for grouping and categorization of plants. The variation occurs in the arrangement of vascular bundles, orientation of xylem and phloem in the bundle, nature and origin of secondary tissue and leaf trace development. It is well known fact that there are close relation between the morphological characters and anatomical structure of the same individual. In case of dicotyledonous plants vascular bundles are arranged in a ring but in monocotyledons scattered vascular bundles are found in the stem. The anatomical criteria is one of the reliable basis of plant classification.

Environmental conditions also plays vital role in development and evolution of plants. This has been noted that same plants grown in varied ecological conditions, such variations should not be taken into consideration while determining new texa. To tackle the effect of environment, genetically similar plants should be grown in different environment and variations are noticed. This methods are helpful in elimination of genetically uniform plant differ in morphological feature. The above mentioned criteria are taken into consideration for categorization or grouping of plants. The system of classification is being discussed in this chapter.

Units of Classification

Species

The science of taxonomy started with the collection and characterization of plants. A species is a group of individuals of one and the same kind. Eventually, they resemble one another in almost all important morphological characters both vegetative and reproductive. So clearly that they may be derived from the same parents.

Genus

The concept of arising definite name for any particular individual was formulated on basic assumptions of genus (by avoiding duplication). The earlier authentic record of genus is as early as in 1532 by Otto Brunfels. Similarly, in floral morphology, fruits, root, leaves, seed, seedling, embryo are usually considered as criteria for determination of genus. A genus is a collection of species bears a close resemblance to one another in the morphological characters of the floral or reproductive parts.

Family

A family is a group of genera which show general structural resemblance with one another mainly in their floral organs. Genera are grouped together into higher taxon, the family. Dimensions of the family ranges from single genus to hundreds of genera.

Order

It is a group of families having similar evolutionary trend and some general resemblance form order.

System of Classification

There are millions of plants showing resemblances as well as differences but none of them are similar. The classification of plants are mind puzzling act. Plants showing morphological resemblance may not necessarily to belong in similar group. Evolution process and environmental stability significantly influence plant morphology. Basic taxonomic grouping based on morphological peculiarities alone, plants were classified on the basis of their chemical composition under the aegis of chemotaxonomy or biochemical systematics, cytogenetically analysis and PCR or DNA finger printing. However, the earlier system of classification proposed since the period of Theophtastus are having historical importance. The major system of classification was

1. Artificial system based on numerical classification
2. Natural system based on form relationship.
3. Phylogenetic system based on evolutionary and genetic relationship.

Artificial System of Classification

In this system of classification only one or at most few characters are selected deliberately and plants are arranged into groups according to such characters. This system of classification was artificial, since it was based on certain pre

- selected characters, but due to its simplicity persisted for quite a long time. *Carolus Linnaeus*, the great Swedish naturalist and physician, was most prominent feature in systematic botany during 1707-1778. He was the originator of the sexual system of classification, he recognized 24 classes, on the basis of the number, union, length and certain other characters of stamens, classes were divided into orders. Plants with one stamens placed in class Monandria, with two indiandria, three- triandria, tetrandria (4 stamens), pentandria (5 stamens) and polyandria (20 or more stamens). Class Didynamia (Didynamous stamens), Monadelphia (stamens in one bundle), Diadelphia (two bundles), Polyadelphia (stamens in more than one bundles), plants with syngenesious stamens (anther united) kept in class syngenesia, while as the class monoecious and dioecious includes monoecia dioecia plants respectively. Class polygamia included all polygamous plants and non flowering plants (Algae, fungus, bryophyta, Ferns, lichens) placed in the large class Cryptogamia.

Carolus Linnaeus (Carl VonLinne) was the founder of the modern concept of classification and known as *Father of Modern Botany*. His valuable contributions to the subject are *Genera Plantarum* (1754); *Species Plantarum* (1753); *Hortus Uplandicus* (1732). He discussed all above (24 classes) in his *Genera plantarum* Linnaeus system of classification based on the numerical relationship between floral organs as male and female ones. This system based more on the dissimilarities rather than similarities. He has presented fragments of natural system of classification in his *Philosophy Botany* (1751), in 67 natural orders of the rank of modern day families and also said that much work still to be done. On these lines, before suggesting the natural system of classification for plants. But he could not presented the concrete basis to distinguish the different characters for orders. The theory of evolution was not clear during the Linnaeus era.

Linnaeus was the first Botanist to use the binomial nomenclature extensively in the work entitled *Species Plantarum* which was published in 1753. His system of classification was quite satisfactory for certain, families but mostly unrelated plants were placed together and closely related plants were separated have been the negative aspect of artificial system of classification.

Natural System of Classification

In natural system of classification, all the important characters are taken into consideration and plants are classified according to their related characteristics. All the modern system of classification is natural and they supersede the artificial ones by the fact that they give a true idea about the natural relationship existing between different plants and their evolution. *Augustin Pyrame de Candolle* (1778-1841) published his classical work. "*Theorie elementaire de la batanique* was published in 1813, he described that the relationship among the plants can be best ascertained by comparative morphology and physiological characteristics and defined the principles of natural system. Further John Lindley (1799-1815) who published "*Introduction to the natural orders of plants*" in 1830 was universally recognized in America and Great Britain.

The concept of natural system of classification has changed and now recommends formulation of texa and placement of individuals in district taxa on the basis of maximum number of phenotypic characters and phylogenitic (evolutionary) evidence. Two botanist George Bentham (1800-1884) and Sir Joseph D. Hooker elaborated the natural system of classification in his *Genera Planatrum* book published in 3 volumes. This book still continues to serve as standard and much consulted work. Brief Bentham and Hookers system of classification may be summarized as follows. He classified the plants into group (Angiosperm, Gymnosperm), sub-groups, (Dicotyledons, Monocotyledons),

Division, Series, Order and finally Family. His overall classification based on floral organs their numbers and arrangements brief summary of *Bentham and Hooker's system of classification*, as described by Nath (1987) and Shukla and Mishra (1979).

Phanerogams (seed plants)

Groups : Angiosperm Gymnosperm

Sub groups : Dicotyledons Monocotyledons

Divisions: Polypetalae (Petals which constitute corolla is free)

Series (A) Thalamiflorae (Petals stamens hypogynous carpels mostly free, ovary superior)

Orders (Cohort) (i) Ranales

Families:- Ranuculaceae, Dilleniaceae, Calycanthaceae, Magnoliacaceae, Anonaceae, Menispermaceae, Berberideae, Nymphacea

ii) Parientales - Sarraceniaceae, Papaveraceae, Cruciferae, Capparideae, Resedaceae, Cistineae, Violarieae, Canellaceae, Bixineae

iii) Polygalinae- Pittosporeae, Tremandreae, Polygaleae, Vochysiaceae.

iv) Caryophyllinae: Frankeniaceae, Tremandreae, Portulaceae, Tamariscineae.

v) Guttiferales: Elatineae, Hypericineae, Guttiferae, Ternstroemiacea, Dipterocarpeae, Chlaenaceae.

vi) Malvales - Malvaceae, Sterculiaceae, Tiliaceae.

Series **(B) Disciflorae**: (Sepals free from ovary, ovary superior, stamens usually definite, inserted on disc like ring.)

Orders vii) Geraniales (it is a large order containing 11 families)

Families:- Lineae, Humiriaceae, Malpighiaceae, Zygophyleae, Geraniaceae, Rutaceae, Simarubeae, Ochnaceae, Burseraceae, Meliaceae, Chailletiacea,

viii) Olacales (a cupular or annular disc always present) Olacineae, Ilicineae, Cyrilleae.

ix) Sapindales- Sapindaceae, Sabiaceae, Anacardiaceae, Coriarieae, Maringeae

x) Celastrales - Celastrineae, stackhousieae, rhamneae, Ampelideae.

Series (C) Calyciflorae- Petals and stamens, perigynous ovary, sometimes inferior, the gynoecium often enclosed due to growth of floral axis.

Orders : (xi) - Rosales,

Families : Connaraceae, Leguminoseae, Rosaceae, Saxifrageae, Crasulaceae, Droceraceae, Hamamelideae, Bruniaceae, Halorageae.

Order (Cohort) xii) : Myrtales.

Families : Rhizophoraceae, Combretaceae, Myrtaceae, Melastomaceae, Lythrarieae, Onagrarieae,

Passiflorales (xiii) Syncarpous, inferior ovary.

Families: Samydaceae, Loaseae, Turneraceae, Passifloreae, Cucurbitaceae, Begoniaceae, Datisceae.

Ficoidales (xiv) syncarpous inferior ovary, rarely superior, Cacteae, Ficoideae

Umbellales (xv) syncarpous inferior ovary rarely superior, Umbelliferae, Araliaceae, Cornaceae.

Division (II)

Gamopetalae Series (A) Inferae- stamens equal in number to corolla lobes and ovary inferior.

Order (cohort) (i) Rubiales (stamens epipetalous)

Families: Caprifoliaceae, Rubiaceae.

(ii) Asterales (stamens adanate to the corolla tube)

Families: Valerianeae, Dipsaceae, Calycereae, Compositeae.

iii) Companales Stylidieae, Goodenovieae, Caompanulaceae,.

Series (B) Heteromerae- Ovary usually superior, stamens as many as the lobes of

The corolla or more, carpels more than two.

Orders (iv) Ericales (stamens usually double the number of corolla lobes.

Families: Ericaceae, Vaccinieae, Monotropeae, Epacrideae, Diapensiaceae, Lennoaceae,

Order:- iv) Primulales

Families:- Plumbagineae, Primulaceae, Myrsineae,

v) Ebenales

Sapotaceae, Elenaceae, Styraceae.

Series (c) Bicarpellatae: Ovary usually superior number of stamens corresponds with the number of corolla lobes stamens adanate to the corolla tube.

Orders vii) Polymoniales.

Families: Polymoniaceae, Hydrophyllaceae, Boragineae, Convolvulaceae, Solanaceae.

Order vii) Personales

Families:- Scrophularineae, Hydrophyllaceae, Boragineae, Convolvulaceae, Solanaceae.

Order vx) Lamiales-

Families: Myoporineae, Solagineae, Verbenaceae, Labiatae, Plantaginae.

Division III Monochlomydeae

Plants of this division mostly lack of corolla in their flowers, sometimes the perianth lobe is altogether absent. It has eight series but no orders.

Series (i) Curvembryeae- flowers usually perfect number of stamens almost equal to sepals.

Families: Nyctagineae, Illecebraceae, Amarantaceae, Chenopodiaceae, Phytolaceae, Batideae, Polygonaceae.

Series (II) Multiovulatae aquaticae.

Plants are aquatic, ovary syncarpous with numerous ovules

Family: Podestemaeae.

Series (III) Multiovulatae terrestres-

Plants are terrestrial herbs and shrubs, ovary syncarpous with numerous ovules/loculer, Aristolochiaceae, Nepanthaceae, Cytinaceae

Series (IV) Micrombryeae- embryo, ovary small, ovary either apocarpous or syncarpous with single ovule.

Families : Piperaceae, Chloranthaceae, Myristiaceae, Monimiaceae.

Series (V) Daphnales- ovary usually moniocarpous, rarely syncarpous, flower perfect, stamens perigynous, perianth sepaloid in one or two series.

Families: Laurineae, Proteaceae, Thymelaeaceae, Penaeacae, Elaeagnaceae.

Series (VI) Achlamydosporeae

Ovary unilocular with 1 to 3 ovules, seeds without testa, perianth may be seploid or petaloid , plants are mostly parasitic.

Families: Loranthaceae, Santalaceae, Balanophoreae.

Series: (VII) Unisexuales: Perianth absent, flower unisexual ovary syncarpous rarely monocarpellary.

Families: Euphorbiaceae, Balanopseae, Uriticaceae, Plantanaceae, Casuarineae, Juglandeae, leitnerieae, Myricaceae, Capuliferae

Series (VIII) Ordines anomali- flowers are unisexual.

Families: Salicaceae, Lacistemaceae, Empetraceae,

Ceratophylleae.

Sub group: Monocotyledones- mostly herbs, rarely shrubs are tree, stem without pith, vascular bundle open without cambium, leaves large with parallel venation embryo monocotyledonary, fibrus root system with no branching habit.

Series (i) Microspermae- Perianth lobes often petaloid, ovary unilocular, carpels three and parietal ovules many.

Families: Hydrocharideae, Burmanniaceae, Orchideae

Series (ii) Epigyneae- Inner perianth lobes always potaloid with superior and free ovary.

Families: Scitamineae, Bromeliaceae, Haemodoraceae, Irideae, Taccaceae, Amaryllideae, Diascoreaceae.

Series (iii) Coronarieae;

Families: Roxburghiaceae, Liliaceae, Pontederiaceae, Philydraceae, Xyrideae,Mayaceae, Commelinaceae, Rapateaceae.

Series (iv) Calycinae- Perianth is seploid and small, the ovary is free.

Families: Flagellarieae, Juncaceae, Palmae.

Series (V): Nudiflorae- Perianth either absent or very tiny like hair or scales, superior ovary.

Families: Pandoneae, Cyclanthaceae, Typhaceae, Aroideae, Lemnaceae.

Series (VI) Apocarpae- Perianth 1-2 seriate, or lacking, superior ovary. Carpel mostly one and the seeds are exalbuminious .

Families: Triurideae, Alismaceae, Naiadaceae,

Series (viii) Glumaceae- flowers sessile, arranged in heads or spikelets with bracts. Perianth either absent or very minute ovary unilocular or multilocular with one ovule in each locules seed always endospermic.

Families: Eriocauleae, Centrolepideae, Cyperaceae, Restiaceae, Gramineae.

III. Phylogenetic Systems of Classification

The term phylogeny was coined by Ernst Heinrich Haeckel in 1886 is the evolution of a genetically related group of organism. With the acceptance of theory of evolution the taxonomist began to rearranged plant families in an effort to place closely related plants on the basis of their ancestral belongings. Due to several difficulties and limitations *viz* lack of knowledge about pre historic forms to enable the plant taxonomist to determine from the evolutionary point of view, no taxonomist has succeeded for developing a truly phylogenetic system because which characters are primitive and which are advanced.

Most widely accepted phylogenetic system of classification continues to be that proposed by Adolph Engler. Engler's classification was adopted widely in Europe and America. Engler's classification is chiefly based on the De Jussieu and Eichlor's system with modification in the status of order and families. For the arrangements of orders and families Engler's classification is infact a model. The distinct feature of this classification was original description of the individuals and inclusion of large number of plants with key for identification. In the Engler's system, the families of higher vascular plants are arranged according to the advancing complexity of flower. In primitive forms, flowers are naked and contain a bract like perianth and advanced forms shows a differentiation in calyx and corolla. The present existing forms are result of continuous course of evolution, which has documented by merely a fragmentary fossil record and exact evidence are obscure. According to Engler opinion, all the flower parts viz sepals, petals, carpels and stamens were evolved independently in any flower. They recognised 280 families of flowering plants including those of gymnosperms. The forward step in the Engler and Prantl's system was the amalgamation of the polypetalae and apetalae of Bentham and Hooker's system under single group Archichlamydeae and in monocotyledons taking precedence of dicotyledonones. Engler's system had certain demarite such as in archichlamydeae, apetalous families composing the group Amentiferae or catkin bearer (Piperaceae, Selicaceae, Betulaceae, Fagaceae, Urticaceae etc) are considered as the most primitive and precede petaliferous families as Ranunculaceae and Magnoliaceae. Monocotyledons are treated more primitive group. Among the individual of monocotyledons Grasses and Pandanales represent more primitive than orchid having well developed flower. The classification of Engler's and Pranl's is as follows (Ravindra Nath, 1987).

Phanerogams Siphonogams (seed forming plants)

Groups Angiosperms

class Monocotyledoneae (11 orders 46 families)

Dicotylldoneae (44 orders and 261 families)

Sub class Archichlamydeae (Apetalae)

Metachlamydeae (Sympetalae, corolla is united

Gymnosperm (plants having naked seeds)

i) Cycadofilicales
ii) Cycadales
iii) Bnennettitales
iv) Ginkgoales
v) Coniferales
vii) Cordaitales
viii) Gnetales

Class I:- Monocotyledoneae

order (1):- Pandanales

families:- Typhaceae, Pandanaceae, Sparganiaceae

order (2) Helobiae

families:- Potamogetonaceae, Najadaceae, Aponogetonaceae, Scheuchzeriaceae, Alismaceae, Butomaceae, Hydrocharitaceae.

Order (3):- Triuridales.

Families:- Tiriuridaceae.

Order (4):- Glumiflorae

Familirs:- Gramineae, Cyperaceas

Order (5):- Principes

Family: - Palmae

Order (6) Synanthae

Family:- Cyclanthaceae

Order (7) :- Spathiflorae

Families:- Araceae, Lemnaceae.

Order (8) :- Farinosae

Families:- Flagellariaceae, Restionaceae, Centrolepidaceae, Mayacaceae, Xyridaceae, Pontederiaceae, Eriocaulaceae, Rapateaceae, Cyanastraceae, Philydraceae, Bromeliaceae, Commelinaceae.

Order (9):- Liliflorae

Families:- Juncaceae, Stemonaceae, Liliaceae, Amaryllidaceae, Velloziaceae, Haemodoracea Dioscoreaceae, Taccaceae, Iridaceae.

Order (10):- Scitamineae.

Families:- Musaceae, Zingiberaceae, Cannaceae,

Moxantaeae

Order (11):- Microspermae

Families:- Burmanniaceae, Orchidaceae.

Class 2: Dicotyledoneae

Sub class (A): Archichlamydeae, Perianth abscent, corolla polypetalous. This subclass Contain 30 orders (cohort) and 201 families.

Order (1):- Verticillatae

Family:- Casuarinaceae

Order (2) Piperales

Families:- Saururaceae, Piperaceae, Chloranthaceae, Lacistemaceae.

Order (3) Salicales

Family: Salicaceae.

Order (4) :- Gorryales

Family:- Garryaceae.

Order (5):- Myricales

Family:- Myricaceae.

Order (6):- Balanopsidales

Family:- Bolanopsidaceae.

Order (7):- Leitneriales

Family:- Leitneriaceae.

Order (8):- Juglandales.

Family:- Juglandaceae.

Order (9):- Batidaceae

Family:- Batidaceae.

Order (10) Julianiales

Family:- Julianiaceae.

Order (11):- Fagales.

Family:- Betulaceae, Fagaceae.

Order (12):- Uritcales

Families:- Ulmaceae, Moraceae, Urticaceae.

Order (13):- Proteales.

Family:- Proteaceae.

Order (14) Santalales

Families:- Myzodendraceae, Santalaceae, Opiliaceae, Grubbiaceae., Olaceae, Octoknematacea.

Order (15) : Aristolochiales

Families: Aristolochiaceae, Rafflesiaceae, Hydnoraceae.

Order (16):- Polygonales

Family:- polygonaceae.

Order (17):- Centrospermae

Families:- Chenopodiaceae, Amranthaceae, Nyctaginaceae, Cynocrambaceae, Phytolecaceae Caryophllaceae. Basellaceae, Aizoaceae, Portulaceae

Order(18):- Ranales

Families:- Nymphaceae, Ceratophyllaceae, Trochodendraceae, Cercidiphyllaceae, Ranunculaceae, Lardizabalaceae, Berberidaceae, Menispermaceae, Magnoliaceae, Calycanthaceae, Lactoridaceae, Anonaceae, Eupomatiaceae, Lauraceae, Hernandiaceae.

Order (19) :- Rhoeadales

Families:- Papaveraceae, Capparidaceae, Cruciferae, Resedaceae, Tovariaceae, Moringaceae.

Order (20) : Sarraceniales

Families:- Sarraceniaceae, Nepenthaceae, Droseraceae,

Order (21):- Rosales

Families:- Podostemaceae, Rosaceae, Tristichaceae, Hydrostachyaceae,Crassulaceae, Cephalotaceae, Saxifragaceae, pittosporaceae, Brunelliaceae, Cunoniaceae, Myrothamnaceae, Bruniaceae ,.Hamamelidaceae, Eucommiaceae, Platanaceae, Crossosomataceae, Connaraceae, Leguminoceae.

Order (22): Pandales

Family :- Pandaceae.

Order(23): Geraniales

Families:- Geraniaceae, Oxalidaceae, Tropaeolaceae, Linaceae, Humiriaceae, Linaceae, Humiriaceae, Simarubaceae, Burseraceae, Meliaceae, Malpighiaceae, Trigoniaceae, Vochysiaceae, Tremandraceae, Polygalaceae, Dichapetalaceae, Euphorbiaceae, Erythroxylaceae, Zygophyllaceae, Rutaceae, Callitrichaceae.

Order (24) Sapindales

Families:- Empetraceae, Coriariaceae, Anacardiaceae, Limnanthaceae, Buxaceae, Cyrillaceae, Corynocarpaceae, Pentaphylaceae, Corynocarpaceae, Aquifoliaceae, Celastraceae, Hippocrateaceae, Salvadoraceae, Staphyeaceae, Stackhousiaceae, Icacinaceae, Sabiaceae, Melinthaceae, Balsaminaceae, Saindaceae, Aceraceae, Hiocastanaceae.

Order(25) Rhamnales

Families:- Rhamnaceae, Vitaceae.

Order (26) Malvales

Families:- Elaeocarpaceae, Chlaenaceae, Tiliaceae, Gonystilaceae, Malvaceae, Sterculiaceae, Scytopetalaceae. Bombacaceae.

Order(27) Parietales

Families:- Dilleniaceae, Eucryphiaceae, Ochnaceae., Caryocaraceae, Maregraviaceae, Quiinaceae, Theaceae, Dipterocarpaceae, Frankeniaceae, Bixaceae, Winteraceae, Flacourtiaceae, Passifloraceae, Datiscaceae, Caricaceae, Turneraceae, Ancistrocladaceae, Guttiferae, Elatinaceae, Tamaricaceae, Begonianceae, Loasaceae, Achariaceae, Malesherliaceae, Stachyuraceae, Violaceae, Cochlospermaceae, Cistaceae.

Order(28): Opuntiales

Family:- Cactaceae.

Order (29):- Myrtiflorae.

Families:- Geissolomataceae, Penaeaceae, Cynomoriaceae, Haloragidaceae, Combretaceae, Nyssaceae, Lecythidaceae, Sonneratiaceae, Elaeagnaceae, Oliniaceae, Thymelaceae, Lythraceae, Punicaceae, Rhizophoraceae, Alangiaceae, Myrtaceae, Hippuridaceae, Onagraceae.

Order (30):- Umbelliflorae.

Families:- Araliaceae, Cornaceae, Umbelliferae.

Sub class (B) Metachlamydeae- corolla is united perianth in two whorls, stamens twice of the petals.

Order (1) :- Ericales.

Families:- Clethraceae, Pyrolaceae, Lennoaceae, Ericaceae, Epacridaceae, Diapensiaceae.

Order (2):- Primulales.

Families:- Theophrastaceae, Primulaceae, Mysinaceae.

Order (3):- Plumbaginales.

Familiy:- Plumbaginaceae.

Order (4):- Ebenales.

Families:- Sapotaceae, Ebenaceae, Symplocaceae, Styracaceae.

Order (5) :- Contortae.

Families:- Oleaceae, Apocynaceae, Gentianaceae, Asclepiadaceae.

Order (6):- Tubiflorae

Families:- Convolvulaceae, Polemoniaceae, Verbenaceae, Hydrophyllaceae, Boraginaceae, Nolanaceae, Labiatatae, Solanaceae, Scrophulariaceae, Bignoniaceae, Pedaliaceae, Martyniaceae, Orobancaceae, Gesneriaceae, Columelliaceae, Lentibulariaceae, Myoporaceae, Globulariaceae, Acanthaceae, Myoporaceae, Phrymaceae,

Order (7):- Plantaginales.

Family:- Plantaginaceae.

Order (8):- Rubiales.

Families:- Valerianaceae, Rubiaceae, Caprifoliaceae, Adoxaceae, Dipsaceae.

Order (9) :- Cucurbitales.

Family:- Cucarbitaceae.

Order (10):- Campanulatae.

Families:- Campanulaceae, Brunoniaceae, Stylidiaceae, Calyceraceae, Compositae.

Hutchinson System of Classification

John Hutchinson (1926-34) suggested most recent system of classification of flowering plants on the basis of phylogenetic and published *"The Families of flowering Plants"* in the year 1926, 1959 and 1973. His system was revised by his son with little modulations in the affinities of certain taxa. Hutchinson assumed dictoyledones more primitive than monocotyledones. The families in these two groups are arranged in increasing order of their specialization of the flower associated characters. He deleted groups like polypetalae, Calyciflorae, Archichlamydeae, Gamopetalae and Apetalae as these are based on artificial characters. Further he suggested angiosperms be classified into two evolutionary lines one herbaceous beginning with Ranales comprising herbaceae and second woody perennials representing Magnoliales forming Lignoceae.

Salient Features of Hutchinson Classification

(i) Dicotyledones have been primarly divided into two main divisions.

(ii) Trees and shrubs considered more primitive than herbs and older than climber in any families, perennials are older than biennials and annuals.

(iii) Simple leaf are primitive than compound leaf.

(iv) Unisexual flowers are advanced than bisexual.

(v) Monoecious plants are more primitive than dioecious plants.

(vi) Hypogyny, epigyny, perigyny have advanced gradually, similarly apocarpous more primitive than syncarpous, endospermic embryo more primitive than seed devoid of endosperm. Separate anthers and numerous stamens are primitive.

Hutchinson did not considered the cytological and anatomical evidence for establishment of his classification basis and given more weightage to phyletic concept. There was no consensus for most primitive families of Angiosperm. The beginning of current century faced the problem to consider catkin bearing Amentiferae, (Engler and Prantl) of Magnoliaceae (Bentham and Hooker) as most primitive of angiosperms. Bessey (1897) and Hallier in many papers opposed Engler and Prantl for first time followed by findings of Arber and Parkin (1907) presented in his paper "*The Origin of Angiosperm*". These taxonomist emphasized Magnoliaceae as the primitive most family of Angiosperms.

Hutchinson system of classification could not received much recognition, though revision of monocot has been accepted. He recognized 105 natural orders (Cohorts) and 411 families. Brief summary of Hutchinson classification.

← Cryptogam — Phanerogams

Phylum : Gymnosperm Angiosperm

Phylum: Angiosperm

Sub phylum : Dicotyledones Monocotyledones

Division Lignosae Herbaceae

Orders (1):- Magnoliales

Families:- Magnoliaceae, Illiciaceae, Winteraceae, Canellaceae, Schisandraceae, Himantandraceae, Cercidiphyllaceae.

Order (2):- Annonales

Families:- Annonaceae, Eupomatiaceae

Order (3)- Laurales

Families:- Monimiaceae, Austrobaileyaceae, Lauraceae, Trimeniaceae, Hernandiaceae, Gomortegaceae, Myristicaceae.

Order (4):- Dilleniales.

Families:- Dilleniceae, Connoraceae, Crossomataceae, Brunelliaceae.

Order (5):- Coriariales.

Family:- Coriariaceae.

Order(6):- Rosales.

Families:- Rosaceae, Dichapetalaceae, Calycanthaceae.

Order (7):- Leguminales.

Families:- Caesalpiniaceae, Mimosaceae, Papilionaceae.

Order (8):- Cunoniales.

Families:- Pterostemonaceae, Cunoniaceae, Philadelphaceae, Hydrangeaceae, Oliniaceae, Greyiaceae, Baueraceae, Crypteroniaceae.

Order (9):- Styracales

Families:- Lissocarpaceae, Styraceae, Symplocaceae.

Order (10):- Araliales.

Families:- Cornaceae, Alangiaceae, Garryaceae, Nyssaceae, Araliaceae, Caprifoliaceae.

Order(11) Hamamelidales

Families:- Tetracentraceae, Myrothamnaceae, Platanaceae, Hemamelidaceae, Stachyuraceae, Buxaceae, Daphniphyllaceae, Bruniaceae.

Order (12):- Salicales

Family:- Salicaceae.

Order (13):- Leitneriales

Family:- Leitneriaceae.

Order (14):- Myricales.

Family:- Myricaceae

Order (15):- Balanopales.

Family:- Balanopaceae

Order (16):- Fagales

Families:- Betulaceae, Fagaceae, Corylaceae.

Order (17):- Juglandaceae.

Families:- Juglandaceae, Rhoipeteaceae, Picrodendraceae,

Order (18):- Casuarinales

Family:- Casuarinaceae

Order (19):- Urticales

Families:- Urticaceae, Moraceae, Cannabaceae, Barbeyaceae.

Order (20):- Bixales.

Families:- Bixaceae, Cistaceae, Flacourtiaceae, Cochlospermaceae, Lacistemaceae.

Order (21):- Thymelaeales

Families:- Thymelaceae, Nyctaginaceae, Penaeaceae, Gonystylaceae.

Order (22):- Proteales

Family:- Proteaceae.

Order (23):- Pittosporales

Families:- Pittosporaceae, Byblidaceae, Vivianiaceae, Tremandraceae, Stegnospermetacea

Order (24):- Capparales.

Families:- Capparaceae, Moringaceae, Tovariaceae.

Order (25):- Tamaricales.

Families:- Tamaricaceae, Frankeniaceae, Fouquieriaceae,

Order (26):- Violales.

Family:- Violaceae.

Order (27):- Polygalales

Families:- Polygalaceae, Krameriaceae, trigoniaceae, Vochysiaceae.

Order (28):- Loasales

Families:- Loasaceae, Turneraceae.

Order (29):- Passiflorales

Families:- Passifloraceae, Malescherbiaceae, Achariaceae,

Order (30):- Cucurbitales

Families:- Cucurbitaceae, Begoniaceae, Caricaceae, Datiscaceae.

Order (31):- Cactales

Family:- Cactaceae

Order (32):- Tiliales

Families:- Dirachmaceae, Scytopetalaceae, Tiliaceae, Sterculiaceae, Bombacaceae, Peridiscaceae

Order(33):- Malvales

Family: - Malvaceae.

Order (34):- Malpighiales.

Families:- Malpighiaceae, Linaceae, Ixononthaceae, Humiriaceae, Irvingiaceae, Huaceae, Zygohyceae Lepidobotryaceae, Balanitaceae.

Order (35) Euphorbiales.

Familiy:- Euphorbiaceae.

Order (36):- Theales.

Families:- Theaceae, Saurauiaceae, Actinidiaceae, Bonnetiaceae, Pentaphylaceae, Caryocaraceae, Medusagynaceae.

Order (37):- Ochnales

Families:- Ochnaceae, Strasburgeriaceae, Sarcolaenaceae, Sphaerosepalaceae, Dipterocarpaceae, Ancistrocladaceae,

Order (38):- Ericales

Families:- Ericaceae, Pyrolaceae, Epacridaceae, Clethraceae, Vacciniaceae. Diapensiaceae, Monotropaceae, Lennoaceae.

Order (39):- Guttiferales.

Families:- Clusiaceae, Eucryphiaceae, Quiinaceae, Hypericaceae,

Order (40):- Myrtales.

Families:- Myrtaceae, Nepoleonaeaceae, Rhizophoraceae, Sonneratiaceae, Punicaceae, Combretaceae, Melastromataceae.

Order (41):- Celastrales.

Families:- Pandaceae, Koeberliniaceae, Cneoraceae, Salvadoraceae, Aquifoliaceae, Icacinaceae, Acxtoxicaceae, Goupiaceae, Hippocrateaceae, Erythropalaceae, Celastraceae. Syphonodontaceae, Scyphostegiaceae. Empetraceae, Pentadilandraceae

Order (42)- Olacales

Families:- Olacaceae, Opiliaceae, Octokenemaceae, Aptandraceae, Dipentodontaceae. Medusandraceae.

Order (43)- Santanlales.

Families:- Loranthaceae, Grubbiaceae, Santalaceae, Myzodendraceae, Balanophoraceae,

Order (44)- Rhamnales

Families:- Rhamnaceae, Vitaceae, Elaeagnaceae, Heteropyxidaceae.

Order (45)- Myrsinales.

Families:- Myrsinaceae, Theophrastaceae, Aegicerataceae,

Order (46)- Ebenales

Families- Ebenaceae, Sapotaceae, Sarcospermataceae.

Order (47)- Rutales

Families- Rutaceae, Simaroubaceae, Burseraceae, Averrhoaceae.

Order (48)- Meliales.

Family- Meliaceae

Order (49)- Sapindales.

Families- Sapindaceae, Podoonaceae, Sabiaceae, Anacardiaceae, Aceraceae, Akaniaceae, Hippocastanaceae, Staphyleaceae, Julianiaceae, Didiereaceae, Meliathaceae.

Order (50)- Loganiales.

Families- Loganiaceae, Potaliaceae, Buddlejaceae, Spigeliaceae, Strychnaceae, Oleaceae, Antoniaceae.

Order (51)- Apocynales.

Families- Apocynaceae, Plocospermataceae, Periplocaceae, Asclepiadaceae,

Order (52)- Rubiales.

Families- Rubiaceae, Dialypetalanthaceae.

Order (53)- Bignoniales

Families- Bignoniaceae, Cobaeaceae, Pedaliaceae, Martyniaceae.

Order (54)- Verbenales

Families- Verbenaceae, Stilbaceae, Phrymataceae, Ehretiaceae, Dicrastylidaceae.

Division II Herbaceae

Orders (1)- Ranales

Families- Ranunculaceae, Paeoniaceae, Helleboraceae, Nymphaceaceae, Podophyllaceae, Ceratophyllaceae, Cabombaceae.

Order (2)- Berberidales

Families- Sargerntodoxaceae, Lardizabalaceae, Menispermaceae, Nandinaceae, Berberidaceae, Circaeasteraceae

Order(3)- Aristolochiales

Families- Aristolochiaceae, Hydnoraceae, Ruffeasiaceae, Nepenthacea

Order (4)- Piperales

Families- Piperaceae, Saururaceae, Chloranthaceae

Order (5)-Rhoeadales

Family- Papaveraceae, Fumariaceae

Order(6)- Cruciales (Brassicales)

Families- Cruciferae, Cleomaceae

Order (7)- Resedales.

Family:- Resedaceae.

Order (8)-Caryophyllales

Families- Caryophyllaceae, Elatinaceae, Molluginaceae, Aizoaceae, Portulaceae.

Order (9)- Polygonales

Families- Polygonaceae, Illecebraceae.

Order (10):- Chenopodiales

Families- Chenopodiaceae, Barbeuiaceae, Phytolaceae, Gyrostemonaceae, Bataceae, Amranthaceae, Agdestidaceae,

Petiveriaceae, Theligonaceae, Basellaceae.

Order(11) Lythrales

Families- Lythraceae, Onagraceae, Trapaceae, Halorrhagidaceae, Callitrichaceae

Order (12)- Gentianales

Families- Gentianaceae, Menyanthaceae

Order (13)- Primulales

Families- Primulaceae, Plumbaginaceae

Order (14)- Plantaginales

Family- Plantaginaceae

Order (15)- Saxifragales

Families- Crassulaceae, Cephalotaceae, Saxifragaceae, Vaholiaceae, Donatiaceae, Parnassiaceae, Adoxaceae, Eremosynaceae, Francocaeae

Order (16)-Sarraceniales

Families- Sarraceniaceae, Droseraceae

Order (17)- Podostemales

Families- Podostemaceae, Hydrostachyaceae.

Order (18)- Umbellales

Family- Umbelliferae.

Order (19)- Valerianales

Families- Valerianaceae, Calyceraceae, Dipsacaceae.

Order (20)- Campanales

Families:- Campanulaceae, Lobeliaceae

Order (21):- Goodeniales

Families- Goodeniaceae, Brunoniaceae, Stylidiaceae

Order (22)- Asterales

Family- Compositae

Order (23)- Solanales

Families:- Solanaceae, Convolvulaceae, Nolanaceae

Order (24)- Personales

Families- Scrophulariaceae, Acanthaceae, Gesneriaceae, Orobanchaceae, Lentibulariaceae, Columelliaceae.

Order (25)- Geraniales.

Families- Geraniaceae, Limanthaceae, Oxalidaceae, Tropaeolaceae, Balsaminaceae.

Order (26)- Polemoniales

Families- Polemoniaceae, Hydrophyllaceae, Cuscutaceae.

Order (27)- Boraginales

Family- Boraginaceae.

Order (28)- Lamiales

Families- Myoporaceae, Selaginaceae, Globulariaceae, Labiatae

Sub-Phylum- Monocotyledones

Division:- 1. Calyciferae.

2. Corolliferae

3. Glumiflorae

Orders (1):- Butomales

Families:- Butomaceae, Hydrocharitaceae.

Order (2):- Alismatales

Families:- Alistmataceae, Scheuchzeriaceae, Petrosaviaceae.

Order(3)- Triuridles

Familiy:- Triuridaceae

Order (4):- Juncaginales

Families:- Juncaginaceae, Liliaceae, Posidoniaceae.

Order (5):-Aponogetonales

Families:- Aponogetonaceae, Zosteraceae.

Order(6):- Najadales

Families:- Zannichelliaceae, Najadaceae.

Order (7):- Potamogetonales

Families:- Potamogetonaceae, Ruppiaceae.

Order (8): Commelinales

Families:- Commelinaceae, Cartonemataceae, Flagellariaceae, Mayacaceae.

Order (9):- Xyridales

Families:- Xyridaceae, Rapateaceae.

Order (10):- Eriocauilales

Family:- Eriocaulaceae

Order(11) Bromelliales

Family:- Bromeliaceae.

Order (12):- Zingiberales

Families:- Musaceae, Lowiaceae, Sterlitziaceae, Zingiberaceae, Cannaceae, Morantaceae.

Division 2:- Corroliferae-Calyx and corolla present and are similar size.

Orders (1):- Liliales

Families:- Liliaceae, Trilliaceae, Potentderiaceae,

Tecophilaceae, Ruscaceae, Smilacaceae

Order (2):- Alstroemeiales

Families:- Petermanniaceae, Alstroemeriaceae, Philesiaceae.

Order(3)- Arales

Families:- Araceae, Lemnanceae.

Order (4):-Typhales

Families:- Typhaceae, Sparganiaceae

Order (5):-Amaryllidales

Family:- Amaryllidaceae

Order(6):- Iridales

Family:- Iridaceae

Order (7):- Dioscoreales

Family:- Dioscoreaceae, Stenomeridaceae, Trichopodaceae, Roxburghiaceae.

Order (8): Agavales

Families:- Agavaceae, Xanthorrhoeaceae

Order (9):- Palmales

Familiy:- Palmae.

Order (10):- Pandanales

Family:- Pandanaceae.

Order(11) Cyclanthales

Family:- Cyclanthaceae.

Order (12):- Haemodorales

Families:- Haemodoraceae, Hypoxidaceae, Velloziaceae, Apostasiaceae, Taccaceae, Philydraceae.

Order (13):- Burmanniales

Families:- Burmanniaceae, Thismiaceae, Corsiaceae

Order (14):- Orchidales

Family:- Orchidaceae.

Division III Glumiflorae- Very small perianth present.

Orders (1):- Juncales

Families:- Juncaceae, Thurniaceae, Centrolepidoceae, Restionaceae.

Order (2):- Cyperales

Familiy:- Cyperaceae

Order(3)- Graminales

Family:- Gramiaceae.

Other Systems of Classification

Arnon - L.Takhtajan (1967).

Arnon was famous phylogenetist at Leningrad, Russia, he established evolutionary inter-relationship amongst species. Takhtajan system of classification has been considered most modern system and described in his book *Flora of Armenia.* He use all available information in his classification of morphology, cytology, palynology, anatomy, embryoiogy, cytogenetics, bio-chemistry and palaebotany.

Class:- A Magnoliatae (Dicotyledonous)

Sub-class-

1. Mangoalidea (Rununculaceae)
2. Hamamelidideae.
3. Caryophyllideae (caryophyllaceae)
4. Dilleniidae (Cruciferae, Ericaceae)
5. Rosidae (Rosaceae, Geraniaceae)

6. Asteridae (Compositae, Caprifoliacea)

Class B- Liliatae (Monocotyledonous)

Sub-class-

1. Alismidae
2. Lilidae
3. Commenlinidae (Gramineae)
4. Arecidae

Besides the above mentioned system of classification, few other systems viz Wettstein (modification of Engler's system), Skottsberg of Goteborg (modification of Wettstein) and Oswald Tippo (1942), which is largely based on morphological and anatomical feature. Tippo sub divided the vascular plants into four sub divisions but he did not elaborates his system below the monocotyledons and dicotyledonous. This system is having limited use.

Chapter **3**

System of Nomenclature

Plants are known by common, vernacular or local name assigned by different persons. Plants growing in a particular are named in language spoken in local area, such names are called as vernacular name or common name, but with the expansion of knowledge many and many common names are coming up by which often confusion creates. Many of the common names are mentioned in the historical books of Chinese, Hindus and other people books. In order to avoid confusion and to give universal accepted name of existing plant species, some general principles of universal acceptance had to be adopted. However, professional botanists gradually suggested names to all plants scientific name. The scientific names are unchanged and published in different language. In this effort, a list of standardized plant name has been published in 1923 by American Committee on *Horticulture Nomenclature*. The scientific name was written in Latin as it was popular language at that period; despite the decline of Roman Empire, the Latin continued to be popular among the educated class. However, the Pliny, Portuguese, Spanish and French were also in use. Gradually, Latin was replaced by Italian language.

Objectives to which a name of taxon is permanently attached. When a species is described, a type specimen is designated that serves as a reference point for others to compare their concept of names. It is a system of speech to communicate about individual entities. Nomenclature pertains to scientific naming of a plants being recognized universally without any modification.

Shreff (1940) has stated that international rules are necessity that they are not be tempered with lightly or to be modified frequently to suit the whims of each fresh fraction that happens to gain ascendancy in a botanical congress, the nomenclatural deliberations should look towards rectifying inadequacies and greater stability and less confusion. As per Blake (1949), first code of nomenclature was proposed by Linnaeus in his book *Critica Botanica* in 1937. He emphasized that no name shall be adopted unless given by a true botanist, who is one and know how to preserve the genera of the nature. Confusion in nomenclature still prevails owing to increase in new plants and inadequacy of the generally accepted international rules. A concept of nomenclature appeared in 1813 with the publication of *Theorie Elementaire de la Botanique* by Augustin Pyramus de Candolle, which was first significant work after Linnean period it was tried to remove the confusing existing in nomenclature. The rules of nomenclature as followed presently, are divided into Chapters and section, sections are divided into articles and recommendations. The rules are mandatory and binding. The recommendations are adopted which provide guidance.

The chief objective of taxonomic botany is to determine and impart correct scientific name of a taxon or plant with scientific name world wide communication about any plants is possible without any ambiguity and it must be remained unchanged. Plants names are given in two kind (1) common names- such names are given according to vernacular name and local language eg. Mango, banana, apple, coffee, tea etc.

Scientific name

Scientific names are given to individual entities after a various steps. These names are internationally accepted. The need to give scientific name was felt, for plants, which should be the same all through the world. If terms are not made distinct between different groups in classification, confusion may arise eventually for biological classification, that have universal acceptance, a standard system of nomenclature would eventually be necessary.

History of Nomenclature

There is no record regarding the beginning of the nomenclature. In early Greek and Roman manuscript gave the first hand name information about plants. The scientific name of plant at present time are Latin name, Roman alphabets are used in the name of plants. That is why Latin names were being used before middle of 18th Century, which was problematic hence, the polynomial nomenclature become much troublesome. The first successful attempts to standardized name to classify all known plants was from Linnaeus (1753). Linnaeus, suggested brilliant system of binomial nomenclature where each individual is denoted by two terms. Linnaeus most fundamental object in his classification was the species. The higher level of grouping of species was the genus. He used it a combination of two Latin terms one for genus and one for species. Thus, the binomial nomenclature still use today (Stafleu, 1971). Linnaeus described binomial nomenclature in his book *Species Plantarum* in 1753. Linnaeus nomenclature of scientific naming were very convenient and therefore the idea was universally accepted by the botanist. To obtained international agreement on the issues, International Congress was organized time to time and rules adopted are published in the form of ICBN. A complete scientific name contain three elements (1) a genus name (ii) species name (iii) a taxonomic author. (e.g. *Mangifera indica* L.) Sometimes, two authors follows a plant name. The use of two authors name is very useful way to trace the nomenclature history of names. Brummitt and Powell (1992) gave the references of taxonomic author abbreviations that is listed in many standard instructions to author of the scientific journal. These references are helpful in description of many crops name, still many authors are using in proper references of name. New references have been provided by Wiersma and Leon (1999); Hanelt, (2001) are properly listing species names of crop plants to help remove this problems. Heiser and Janick's was of opinion to eliminate taxonomic author in journal.

Botanist was of the opinion that nomenclature should be as stable as possible and may not influence with new classification. De Candolle (1867) developed a set of nomenclature rules which led to the first edition of the *Regles de la Nomenclature Botanique*, later editions as ICBN (International Code of Botanical Nomenclature). The ICBN revised every after six years based on consensus (IBC). In this regard, the last IBC was held in St. Louis, Missouri, in 1999, resulting in the latest editions of the ICBN (Greuter *et al.*,2000) also known as St. Louis Code.

ICBN principles, suggests that how the plants get their names, and how new names are assigned to the species. Spooner and Begihad described the principle of nomenclature of cultivated plants which are incorporated in 76 articles appended with recommendations **Botanical nomenclature** is independent of **Zoological** and bacteriological, virological nomenclatural types. When a species is described, a type specimen needs to be designated that serves as a reference point for other to compare to their concept of names. The nomenclature of taxonomic group is based upon priority of publication. It means that the earliest validity published name is the proper name assigned to a taxon. The ICBN provides a way to avoid name changes based on above mentioned principle, however, name of families genera and species are conserved under rule in case anyone wish to bring change, one can move petition to have a name conserved by a published proposal in the *Taxon* Journal. The proposal moved to general assembly of International Botanical Congress, and if a majority accepts the proposal the name is added to the list of conserved name of ICBN that are valid despite having violated rules of the code. Conservation is a nomenclatural device that operate within the taxa in which they have been voted upon. For bringing valid change in taxon, it is not necessarily to be academician, or botanist or licensed authority. Anyone can validily publish a new taxon if he satisfy following criteria. i) Provide a description of statement that how the new taxon differ from something similar. ii) designate a type specimen generally a single herbarium specimen affixing the name to the new taxon iiii) follow rules outlined in the ICBN such as using the proper form of a name regarding spelling and do not using name that have been validity published before iv) effectively publish the new name effective publication typically is through peer reviewed scientific taxonomy journal but it is stipulated in the ICBN only as distribution of to the general public or at least to the botanists generally. New Taxon names are made available through indexing services such as the *Gray Card Index,* or the *Index Kewensis Plantarum Phanerogarum is* the comprehensive list of scientific name of seed plants. The publication was started in 1893-95 for the first time from the Royal Botanic Garden, Kew. In its first publication, all scientific names known since the period of Linnaeus were included alphabetically or the *International Plant Name Index* (http:// www.ipni,org/) maintained. Nomenclature of wild and cultivated plants are differ from each other. Cultivated plants are differ to get *fancy names,* and name would have to be limited to botanical Latin names of the species, sub-species or botanical varieties from which the cultivated plants were derived. Differences on the nomenclature was arrived due to the absence of general rule for the nomenclature. The first publication in this regard came in form of *Theroie elementarie de la botanique* by Augustin de Candolle (1813) and followed by another valuable publication *Nomenclature Botanicus* (1812).

Code of Nomenclature

1. Paris Code (1867)

In 1867, Alphonse de Candolle, brings out a publication *Lois de la nomenclature botanique* in which he incorporated original ideas of botanics from world over. He made significant effort to organize an International Congress at Paris in 1867, first organized attempts in the standardized and legislation of nomenclature was made the International Botanical Congress of Paris 1867. About 150 European and Americans Botanist were attended meeting to discuss. This congress passed rules and regulation which was formulated. The laws were principally based on de Candolle's law of Botanical nomenclature. Often few days deliberation it was resolved that these laws as adopted by assembly shall be recommended on the best guide for nomenclature in the plant kingdom. The rules of Paris Code represented on excellent beginning in the right direction but their application revealed numerous discrepancies. At this congress, he expressed all his ideas regarding the nomenclature of plants on the basis of work done in Taxonomy while discussing on Paris Code, much emphasis was laid on author citation. It was suggested that the person who publishes the account for any plants for the first time giving new name to the genus should be considered as the author of scientific name. If the taxon i.e. genus, species is transferred from one genus to another, the name of first author (Authority) is not deleted and written as the specific epithet as parenthesis. When species is transferred from one genus to another genus the first specific epithet is remain intact. Though the rule recommended by A de Candolle were accepted in the Paris Congress but soon many American and European Botanist and some other proposed *Kew Rule* at Kew which was major centers of taxonomic advancement and this rule independent acceptance. In Kew rule, if the species is transferred from one genus to another, the author suggesting the transfer is free to suggest any specific epithet need not necessarily be retained. Later, Kew Rule led to much controversy between British Botanist who supported the rule and continental and American ones who opposed the rule. However, the Kew Rule was followed in the preparation and compilation of the first two volumes of the Index Kewensis. International Congress resolved many problems related to nomenclature. These congress meet periodically and rules regulations and recommendations are published as ICBN. The ICBN published recommendations are universally acceptable.

Rochester's Code

A meeting of botanist was organized in 1892 by Nathanial Lord Briton, Director of the New York Botanic Gardens and formulated by rules referred to as Rochester's Code principally based on the Paris Code. According to this code, when any plant species is transferred from one genus to another genus then the specific epithets carried by the individual and the generic name may be subject to change, in the event of such corrections generic epithet become similar to the specific epithet of the plants. In such case specific epithet is retained and it then becomes a tautonym. It follow strict application of rule of priority (A generic name repeated in specific epithet eg. *Lycopersicon lycopersicon.*

Vienna Code

Taxonomist were anxious about great differences in the nomenclature opinion of the angiosperm. A need was felt to formulate comprehensive rule of nomenclature after above referred meetings. After that, next congress was held at Vienna in 1905, during this congress followers of Rochester Code emphasized on its merits with certain drawbacks. The rules formulated in the Vienna congress were mainly based on the Paris Code. The principle adopted in this congress was *nomina generica* conservenda. Wide uses of any name must be considered valid rather than the name of the same individual published prior to it. After Vienna congress, Rochester code was abandoned.

American Code

American code came in the picture after Vienna code in 1907. It is a modification of Rochester's code. *Gray's Manual of Botany* was published by Asa Gray in 1908 advocating the rules of Vienna Congress. However, American code differ from Vienna Code as it refused to accept the principle of Mamina Generica Conservenda, it refused to accept the latin diagnosis to accompany the name of new taxa and it rejected the repetition of the some binomial for a plant, but this rules never gained international acceptance. The controversy prevailed until 1930, when the Cambridge Congress agreed unanimously to follow Vienna Congress rule and rejection of American Congress was suggested.

Further the Botanical congress was organized in Amsterdam in 1935, the salient features of the Amsterdam code was rejection of principle of *Nomina Specifica Conservenda*. Later on, congress was held in 1940, 1950 and 1959. The congress was held in Edinburg in 1964 and its proceedings were published in 1966 with the name of Edinburg Code.

Brussels Code

Fourth International Congress convened in 1910 at Brussels. Congress accepted the establishment of different points of priority of name of non-vascular plants, type concept proposed in Rochester Code was also recognized. This code also known for bringing of classification of several Vienna Rules of 1905.

Cambridge Code (1955)

The fifth International Botanical Congress held at Cambridge in 1930. This congress was held to short-out the difference between Vienna Rules and American Rules. The code adopted that the application of names of taxonomic group is determined by means of nomenclatural types. This was the Code of nomenclatural types used by the botanist all over the world.

Amsterdam Code (1947)

Sixth International Botanical Congress held at Amsterdam in 1935, some of rules of nomenclature were again subject of discussion. The salient features of this code was that all diagnosis of newly described plants except (bacteria) must be in latin if published after Jan 1, 1935, instead of Jan 1, 1932 as was recorded in the Cambridge Code. Nomenclature rules were chapters and sections further sub divided into articles and recommendations. The article were accepted as mandatory and bindings and recommendations as guidance. This code rejected the establishment of a list of *Nomina Specifica Conservarda.*

Stockholm Code (1952)

At Stockholm, seventh International Botanical Congress was held, this code experienced some minor changes and a few additions to the rules were made. The taxon was incorporated for the first time to designate any taxonomic group. Taxon of any rank below the rank of a species which include the type of the species is to be designated by repeating epithet. A new article on apomicts added and rejection of *Nomina Specifica Conservanda* was adopted.

Paris Code (1956)

Eight International Congress was convened at Paris in July 1954. the committee on the nomenclatorial section decided that the code should be published in English, French and German languages. The main change made was separation of the preamble and principles from the Rules and Recommendations. *Nomina Specifica Rejicienda* was amended and supplemented.

Montreal Code (1961)

Ninth International Botanical Congress was held at Montreal in August 1959. In this code, the proposal concerning the question of possible *Nomina Specifica*

Conservanda was not accepted but was agreed, then an attempt may be made to assess the importance of the problems before the rule is changed. The committee decided to retain the numbers of articles and recommendations of the Paris Code. Hybrid names and some special categories were slightly amended. Special provisions concerning the fossil plants in Paris code were not incorporated in the code but was agreed to include in the body of code where it is concerned. Naming of the fossil plants shall follow the same lines as that of the recent ones was made clear in the code. *Nomina Familiarum Conservanda* was introduced in this Code.

Edinburgh Code (1966)

Tenth International Botanical Congress was held at Edinburgh in August 1964. Article number was not changed as it was in Paris and Montreal Code. Some changes brought in the numbering of Recommendations subsequent to some deletions. Amendments of bi-generic and multi-generic hybrids, *Nomina Familiarian Conservanda* were made and family names of recently discovered *Gymnosperms* were also added.

Leningrad Code (1978)

The Leningrad Code was based upon the decisions reached by the nomenclature section of 12th International Botanical Congress convened at Leningrad in 1975. in this code, the concept of organ-genera was eliminated for fossil plants. The principle of automatic typification was extended above the family level that were based on generic names, however, on priority basis. The code does not apply to the names of organism treated as bacteria. The article 69 was modified as a name be rejected it has been widely and persistently used for a taxon not including its type. The article 70 and 71 of the Seatlle Code dealing with discordant element and monstrosities were deleted but the article numbers were retained as such.

Sydney Code (1983)

Thirteen International Botanical Congress (IBC) was held at Sydney in 1981, August. This code is quite similar to Leningrad Code except numbering scheme introduced in this code makes the reference to these more simple. Conservation of names of species was accepted but was not included in the code. The article dealing with spelling as used by Linneaus (Article 74) was deleted in the code. Article 60 and 61 was remodeled and article 59 and related provisions were thoroughly remodeled and a change in starting point dates in fungi was adopted. The provisions of the hybrids were thoroughly over handed.

Berlin Code (1988)

Berlin Code was adopted in the 14th IBC held at Berlin 1987, supersedes all the earlier codes of the Botanical Nomenclature. In this Code, text was written in English instead of three different languages English, French and German. This code experienced the listing of Appendix III B as *Nominica Specifica Conservanda et rejicienda.* Two article dealing with illegitimate names (Article 66 and 67) were deleted by the Berlin Congress and Recommendation 75 A dealing with gender of generic names in Sydney Code appear as new article (Article 76). Article 7-10 dealing with typification have been revised, five addition regarding rules on types and typification have been incorporated. Changes regarding illegitimate, orthography and naming of hybrids described in this Code.

Seattle Code

The congress held at Seattle in 1969, and its proceedings with the name of Seattle Code published in 1972 by Mr F.A. Stafleu, chairman of Congress. In this congress, major issue was the Tautonymous designation of taxa between genus, species and reorganization of hybrid name. A list of *Nomina Conservenda* was prepared. This code recommends the botanical nomenclature. Separate rules for giving names to the hybrids have been formulated. All scientific names for taxa is based on the priority in publication, and names are written in Latin irrespective of their origin from any language. The rank of taxa is ascending order are species, genus, family, order and classes. Names suggested in contravention of the rules are termed as illegilamate.

International Code of Botanical Nomenclature

This (taxa) were proposed on the basis of evolutionary classification criteria. In this case, basic binomial consists of genus and species ICBM is a mandatory to designate a conserved specimen to which a new species name is permanently linked. In case, taxonomist consider two species to really be one type specimens determine the proper application of competing names in such circumstances **International Code of Botanical Nomenclature** provide rules to determine the proper name and the synonymnized name. Generally, the older name must be used by the principle of priority.

International Code of Nomenclature for cultivated plants (ICNCP) (1958)

First ICNCP was published in 1953 by W.T. Sternwas. It is nomenclature rules for culta (man made intities). Basic binomial consists of a genus name plus a cultivar epithet. In the ICNCP, cultivars are essentially not subject to revision. This presents an alternative mechanism to fix both a cultivar name and its description.

Among the taxonomist, a change in the ICBN have been debated, if concensus will emerged and adopted as such the ICNCP will also be influenced. A unified code for all life nomenclature have been suggested known as *Biocode.*

Bio Code

Presently, there are five codes for nomenclature of organism, all these codes have different rules, creating a degree of confusion in nomenclature across disciplines. Zoologist and Botanist have made vigorous discussions about the virtue of unified code for the nomenclature of the four codes viz i.e. i). International Code of Botanical Nomenclature (ICBN); Greuter *et al;,* 2000) ii) International Code of Nomenclature for Cultivated Plants (ICNCP; Trehane *et al;,*1995) iii) International Code of Zoological Nomenclature (ICZN; Ride *et al;* ,1999) iv) International Code of Nomendlature of Bacteria: Bacteriological code (BC; Lapage *et al;* ,1992).This initiative called as *Bio Code* (Greuter *et al;* 1996, 1997). The new proposed code (*Bio Code*) has not yet been adopted. Though one group of taxonomist argue that the Bio Code would increase nomenclature instability and create confusion by use of new rules and name change (Brummitt, 1996). Biocode would not take up the classification and nomenclature of cultivated plants in direct sense. The ICNCP shall remain independent on the cultivars and their nomenclature will remain intact.

Phylo Code

Phylo Code is the result of advancement of science and technical know how. Like the Bio Code, it is applicable to all organism not just plants knowledge regarding the phylogenetic relationship of all the organism is begining changed rapidly with the expansion of new data arising from molecular systematic and development of computer and computer aided programme. New relationship among angiosperm were demonstrated by DNA sequences of Chloroplast and ribosomal genes. It is intended eventually to treat all group of organism and is organized by a nested set of phylogenetic trees (Cladograms) (Spooner and Berg 2003). De Queiroz and Gauthier (1992, 1994) proposed that a new nomenclatural system was needed to name clades, in which the use of ranked categories, such as genus and family is not mandatory and these categories have no bearing names. In phylogenetic nomenclature, names are to be applied to clades by any one of three criteria. I) node based clade names ii) stem based clade names iii) apomorphy based clade names. In this regard Cantino and Queriroz (2000) Wrote a draft version of the Phylo Code that is advanced for discussion and modifications. Phylocode is differ from the ICBM, as it avoid the rank related problems. The phylo code produces a more logic system for naming clades. However, it would drastically change a nomenclature system that has served a standard reference system and critics claims it could disrupt ties of names of all ranks, even species binomials to the biological literatures. Phylocode addresses critical concerns about nomenclature.

Chapter 4

Systematic Description of Mango

Mango is also known as king of fruit, it has been in cultivation here since pre-historic times. Mango fruits have been an esteemed item of diet and the true subject of great veneration. The tree is part and parcel of the rural life. Besides being used as avenue tree it provides timber, fuel and fodder. This chapter deals with the systematic description of mango.

Botanist Carol Clusices made the first scientific references of mango in 1605, further Bauhin (1623-50) suggested name Mangas and Amba. Bontius in 1658 put forth the name *Mangifera* first time later the tree was referred as the name *Mangifera indica* Ray. *Mangas domestica* Hermann and *Mangas syltica* Rheede, present scientific name was confirmed by Linnaeus in 1753 (*species plantarum*).

Classification

Division-Spermatophyta

Sub-division:- Angiospermae

Class- Dicotyledonae

Order- Sapindales

Family- Anacardiaceae

Other families- Sapindaceae, Melianthaceae, Podoaceae, Didiereaceae, Anacardiaceae, Aceraceae, Hippocastanaceae, Staphyleaceae, Akaniaceae, Julianiaceae, Podoaceae, Saliaceae.

Systematic Position of Family Anacardiaceae as per taxonomist

Bentham and Hooker	**Hutchinson**
Angiosermae (group)	Angiospermae (phylum)
Dicotyledons (sub group)	Dicotyledones (sub phylum)
Polypetalae (Division)	Lignosae (Division)
Disciflorae (series)	Sapindales (order)
Sapindales (order)	Anacardiaceae (family)
Anacardiaceae (Family)	

Engler and Prantle

Angiospermae

Dicotyledonae (class)

Archichlamydeae (sub class)

Sapindales (order)

Anacardiaceae (family)

Salient Feature of Sapindales Order

1. Mostly plant of tree, shrubs or climber type.
2. Grows mostly in tropical and sub-tropical regions.
3. Leaves mostly compound, usually pinnate, rarely digitate, stipulate rarely found.
4. Flower hypogynous or slightly perigynous, often polygamous or unisexual.
5. Sepals 4-5 united imbricate, petals 4-5 mostly present and free.
6. Ovary superior, with 1-2 rarely numerous ovule per locule with axile placentation.
7. Fruits are drupe or berry.

Salient Feature of Family Anacardiaceae

1. Mostly trees or shrubs.
2. Stem or leaves having acrid or milky sap with resin

canal on stem.

3. Leaves alternate, simple or compound, exstipulated, simple pinnate or palmate.
4. Monoecious or dioecious *(Pistacia vera),* flower in panicles and usually pentamerous, actinomorphic, sepals and petals 3-7, stamens free equal to number of petals or twice or less inserted at the base of an annular ring (disc). Ovary single celled and have one ovule fruit usually drupe with stony endocarp.
5. Fruit plants belongs to Anacrdiaceae family *Anacardium occidentale, Pistacia vera, Schinus molle, Spondias pinnata Buchanania latifolia.*
6. Mango belongs to genus *Mangifera* with 65 species Hooker and Jackson (1895), 32 species Engler and Prantle (1897), 41 species (Mukharjee, 1949 a).

On the basis of disc present, mango species can be classified into two groups:-

i) **Disc Prominent**

Mangifera indica

M. coloneura

M. khasiana

M. altissima

M. pentandra

M. sylvatika

ii) **Disc non-prominent**

M. odorata

M. foetida disc non-prominent

M. caesia

Origin of Mango

Mango is native to India (Mukherjee, 1949, 1985) opined that this genus might have originated in the region covering Burma, Siam, Indo-China and Malayan peninsula. The Indo

– Burma region is supposed to be known as Centre of Origin of mango. Apart from *Mangifera indica,* India is also reported to be the name of four other species viz. *Mangifera andmanica, M. khasiana, M. sylvatica,* and *M. camptosperma* (Mukherjee *et al.* 1985). The highest concentration of *Mangifera* species is reported to be in the Malaya peninsula followed by the Sunda Island, and the eastern peninsula and many of the common species being common between them (Mukherjee, 1949 a). Further, Yadav and Rajan (1993) reported important zone of *M. indica* are follows.

i) Humid sub-tropical region (Manipur, Tripura, Mizoram and South Assam)
ii) Chota Nagpur plateau and part of Madhya Pradesh, Bihar and Orissa, Rajmahal hills (Santhal Pargana)
iii) South Madhya Pradesh (Tribal area) adjoining Orissa and Andhra Pradesh.
iv) Dhar Plateau of Madhya Pradesh and adjoining south Rajasthan and Gujarat.
v) Andaman and Nicobar Island.

Important *Mangifera* species with their locations (Mukhrejee 1948 a)

Mangifera duperreana- Vietnam, Siam, (Thailand)
M. Pentendra – Burma, Malaya, Indo-China

M cochinchinensis -	Cochinchina
M lanceolata -	Malaya
M indica -	Indo-Burma
M longipes-	Burma, Malaya, Sunda and Phillipines
M coloneura -	Burma, Siam
M siamensis-	Siam
M sylvatica-	Indo, Burma, Indo-China
M. oblongifolia-	Malacoa, Siam, Indo-China

M. minor-	New Guinea, Celebs, the Solomon Island
M. zeylanica	Ceylon
M. khasiana-	Assam
M. gracilipes-	Malacca
M. camptosperma-	Burma, Siam, Sumatra, Cochinchina (Vietnam)
M. gedebe-	Java
M. microphylla-	Malaya
M. griffithii-	Malaya
M. sclerophylla-	Malaya
M. merillii-	The Philippines
M. baccarii-	Sarawale
M. similes	Sumatra, Java
M. altissima-	Phillipines
M. havilandi-	Sarawale
M. rigida-	Sumatra
M. maingayi-	Malaya
M. longipetiolata-	Malaya
M. quadrifida-	Malaya
M. spathulaefolia-	Borneo
M. timorensis-	Banda, Sumatra, Timor
M. monandra-	Phillipnes
M. andmanica-	The Andaman Islands
M. lagenifera-	Siam
M. macrocarpa-	Malaya, Sunda, Indo China
M. foetida-	Malaya
M. odorata-	Malaya

M. *kemanga-* The Malaya

M. *caesia-* Malaya

M. *superba-* Malaya

Salient feature of *Mangifera indica*

vi) Evergreen, tropical and subtropical trees, 10-40 meter, long lived (300 years), erect or spreading with dense crown and produce several flushes in a years.

vii) Bark in the old trees becomes corcky and split.

viii) Leaves large elliptic, oblong simple, alternate, young leaves have coppery red to green petiole 1-10 cm long, leaves are spirally arranged.

ix) Long taproot with dense from root at surface for feeding purpose.

x) Flowers are small numerous and borne on panicle on terminal position of shoot, however, in Fazili mango variety panicle borne on axillary position. Flowers are minute 5-8 mm in diameter on cymes or branchlets, sub sessile, sweet scented, sepals 5 or rarely 4-7, free concave, yellowish green Petals later becoming pinkish, annular, fleshy, 5 lobed between corolla and androecium. Flowers polygamous, monoecious or staminate or perfect flower.

xi) Mango inflorescence is also arise from axillary buds quite frequently; panicle branched having several hundred tiny flowers. Panicle contains 800-9000 flowers per panicle depending on variety and agro-climatic condition but only 0.1% of flowers matures fruits. Stamens usually five (3-7) inserted on the outer margin of the disc of which one or occasionally two are fertile, a stamens are 2 mm long with pink anther. Pistil abortive in male flower. Flowers may be male and hermaphrodite (andromonoecious) In hermaphrodite flowers the stamens are sessile, fertile, oblique one celled ovary set on disc with lateral style and small simple stigma approximately same length as fertile stamens single anatropous ovule . It is hermaphrodite flowers which set fruit often proper pollination. Initial fruit set depend much on the number of hermaphrodite flower. According to Popenoe (1927) percentage of hermophrodite flower varies from 0.74 to 70 according to the variety(Rumani, have 0.74% hermaphrodite flower to 69.8% in Langra cultivars).

Genetic wealth available in India is very rich and comprise more than one thousand vegetatively propagated varities. Some important cultivars are as follows:

Importance mango varieties

Menaka

It is selected as chance seedling of Gulabkhas at Sabour and was released in 1991 name was given Menaka due to attractive colour. Medium fruit sized 300 g, attractive red blush on yellow background.

Langra

(Banarasi Langra) - Most popular variety grown in India, excellent fruit quality with wider adoptability a, biennial bearing habit; poor keeping quality.

Dashehari

Excellent fruit quality fibre less, very rich source of vitamin C, good keeping and canning quality.

Samer Bahist Chousa

Most delicious fruit very sweet late maturity, good size and attractive colour, poor fruiting trees quite vigorous with strong apical dominance.

Bombay Green

Earliest among commercial type; good blend for mango nector, poor keeping quality.

Alphonso

Highly exportable cultivar, fruit with excellent flavour,

shape, size and colour, very good keeping quality, highly suitable for canning, flavour stable, flesh develop spongy tissue disorder.

Subhash

It is a change seeding of Zardalu, medium sized fruit of attractive yellow colour, good quality.

Bangalora

Early arrival in the market from South India, good yielder with regular bearing.

Fazli

Late maturing cultivar, abnormally big size, inferior quality.

Dushehari-51

It is superior clonal selection of Dushehari from CISH, Lucknow, U.P and was released during 1998. The peculiar feature of this clone is that it bear good crop without off bearing rhythm. It gives yield of 43.4 kg/tree against very poor or no crop on normal Dashehari tree.

Keser

Medium size fruit attractive apricot yellow colour, excellent table with acid sugar level.

Hybrid varities

Varietal wealth of mango is very rich in the country. Improvement through breeding was initiated in 1911, however, systematic hybridization work was started during fourtees. Some important hybrids are as below.

Pusa Surya

It is hybrid of Amrapali and Sensation, evolved from IARI, Pusa in 2002, New Delhi, regular, medium sized, heavy yielder attractive apricot yellow colour peel with reddish ting, good flavour with 10-12 days shelf life at room temperature, suitable for export purpose.

Pusa Arunima

It is progeny of Amrapali and Sensation evolved from Indian Agricultural Research Institute, Pusa, New Delhi, during 2002 suitable for close planting, regular bearing, precocious (fruiting starts 4th years after planting), it is late maturing cultivars.

Ambika

A high yielding, regular bearer, hybrids, medium sized fruit, yellow, firm flesh, suitable for international market.

Mallika

It is progeny of cross between 'Neelumx Dashehari'. It was developed at IARI, New Delhi in 1971, plant semi vigours, medium cropper, regular bearing. Fruit of apricot yeallow olour, weight more than 300 gm, high soluble solid (24^0 Brix) and good keeping.

Amrapali

It was developed at IARI New Delhi in 1978 progeny of Dashehari x Neelum. It is precocious, dwarf, regular and good cropper, fruits are green apricot yellow, medium sized, TSS 22-24^0 Brix, with high carotene content, late maturing suitable for high density plantation.

Ratna

Hybrid of Neelum x Alphonso, developed from RFRS, Vengurla, Maharastra in 1981. Tree moderate, vigorous, precocious, medium size fruit, attractive good shape, firm flesh, free from spongy tissue, deep orange red colour fruit.

Sindhu

It is first seedless, parthenocarpic variety of mango

progeny of Rotna and Alphonso from RFRS, Vengurla, Maharashtra in 1982. Fruit medium size with very thin stone, devoid of kernel and often referred as seedless mango, flesh firm, free from spongy tissue.

Arka Aruna

It is progeny of Banganpalli x Alphonso; dwarf stature, and ideal for backyard planting, large fruit size (500 gm), ,attractive skin colour fibreless, good flavour, regular bearer and free from spongy tissue.

Arka Puneet

Alphonso x Banganpalli, regular bearing habit, fruit medium size (240 gm), attractive aroma and colour. The fruit with good keeping quality, medium season cultivar. This is free from spongy tissue and fruit fly.

Arka Anmol

Alphonso x Janardan Pasand. It is a semi-vigorous type with regular and profilic bearing habit, fruits are medium sized (330 gm) fruit ripening, good golden yellow colour. Excellent keeping quality with excellent sugar acid blend. The fruit is free from spongy tissue disorder.

Arka Neelkiran

Alphonos x Nelum, It is semi-vigrous type with regular bearing habit, late season variety, medium sized (270 g), fruit have attractive red blush, pulp deep yellow in colour, TSS 20^0 Brix, free from spongy tissue disorder.

Konkan Ruchi

It is progeny of Neelum x Alphonso evolved at Regional Fruit Research Station, Vengurla, Maharastra and was released in 1999. It is regular bearing mango variety developed for pickle making, heavy yielder 70 kg/tree with large fruit size (430 g).

PKM 1

It is progeny of Chinaswarnareka x Neelum. This variety was evolved at Fruit Research Station, Periyakulam, Tamil Nadu, regular bearer and yields over 100 kg/tree/year. It bears fruit in clusters, fruits long shaped are sweet to taste.

PMK 2

(Neelum X Mulgoa), regular bearer, large fruit with good quality and sweet taste.

Julie

it is a chance seeding selection, dwarf hybrid popular in Jamaica, flattened fruit, medium size, flesh not completely fibreless, 30-50% hermaphrodite flower, regular bearer.

Sai Sugandh

Developed through crossing between Totapuri and Kesar from MPKV, Rahuri also known as RHR-M-1, precocious and regular in bearing, fruits oblong intermediate in shape, fruit weight 380g, prominent beak, attractive golden colour fruit, very sweet (22.3% TSS).

Other Hybrids

Al Fazli

Alphonso x Fazli, from FRS, Sabour

Sundar Langra- Sundar Pasnd X Langra.

Sabri

(Gulalle khas x Bombai)

Jawahar

(Gulabkhas x Mahmood Bahar)

Swarna Jehangir

(Chinnawarnarekha x Jehangir)

Neelashan

(Neelum x Baneshan)

Neelgoa

(Neelum X Mulgoa)

Neelphonso

(Neelum X Alphonso)

Au Rumani

(Rumani x Mulgoa)

Manjeera

(Rumani x Nelum)

High pulp recovery - Bombay, Alphonso, Langra, Dashehari, Mallika, Pairi, Vanraj.

Colourd Varieties - Sindhuriya (Gulabkhas Red), Zafran, Sardar Rosa, Dori, Husnara, Janardan Pasand, Suvarnarekha, Lal Mulgoa, Vanraj, Sensation, Haden, and Kent.

Elite line for dwarfness - Rumani, Ladavio and Neelam

High total soluble solids - Saheb Pasand, Dashehari, Malliaka, Amrapali.

Chapter 5

Systematic Description of Citrus

Citrus is one of the important crop of world, it is adoptable to wide range of soil and climatic conditions. The area and production have increased many fold in the last three decades. There is a good deal of diversity, in the views of classification of citrus, due to divergent concept about the species. In this chapter, systematic description of citrus have covered.

Classification

Kingdom	-	plant
Division	-	Phanerogams
Sub-Division	-	Angiosperm
Class	-	Dicotyledonae
Order	-	Geraniales
Sub-order	-	Geraniinea
Family	-	Rutaceae
Sub-Family	-	Aurontoideae
Tribe	-	Citrae (3 sub-tribe)
Sub Tribe	-	Citrinae.

Systematic position of Family Rutaceae as per taxonomist:-

Bentham and Hooker	**Engler Prantle**
Angiospermae (group)	Angiospermae

Dicotyledones (sub group)	Dicotyledoneae(class)
Polypetaleae (Division)	Archichlamydeae (S.class)
Disciflorae (series)	Geraniales (order)
Geraniales (order)	Rutaceae (Family)
Rutaceae (Family)	

Hutchinson

Angiospermae (phylum)

Dicotyledones (S.phylum)

Lignosae (Division)

Rutales (order)

Rutaceae (Family)

Salient features of order Geraniales

i) There are 900 species under this order, 60 species found in India.

ii) Trees, shrubs or climbers, rarely herbs.

iii) Leaves often gland dotted, simple or compound, stipules very rarely present.

iv) Flowers hypogynous, perigynous, mostly bisexual, sepals mostly imbricate, 4-5 free, corolla 4-5 free.

v) Stamens are variable in number may be as many as or twice of petals.

vi) Ovary superior syncarpous or subcarpous, style free or connate, ovule 1-2 or numerous seed with or without endosperm.

vii) Fruit berry or capsule or special type of berry hesperidium.

viii) Important families are Rutaceae, Burseraceae, Simaroubaceae, Averrhoaceae

Salient features of family Rutaceae

i) Plants mostly shrub or tree stem erect woody and branched, often thorny. The bark fragment in many cases.

ii) Leaves simple, compound, glandular punctate, mostly opposite. In some citrus species (orange lemon) the first one or two leaves of the bud in young plants get modified into thorns while the bud itself may become a branch.

iii) Disc almost invariably present between the stamens and ovary from annular to tubular or produced into a gynophores or lining the calyx.

iv) Fruit berry, capsule or special berry hesperidium mostly cymose type of inflorescence but sometimes flowers are arranged either in corymb (*Murraya exotica*) or in racemes (*Citrus medica*).

v) Stamens are variable in number equal or twice of petals, stamens free or united in irregular bundle.

vi) Gynoecium - mostly 4-5 carpellary, syncarpous, superior, 4-5 locules, sometimes the carpels are free towards the base and united above or rarely altogether free, axial placentation. In *Feronia* genus, the ovary is syncarpous with several parietal placentations.

vii) Style free or connate.

viii) Seed with or without endosperm, straight or often curved embryo, rarely winged, often polyembryony.

Other fruit plants belong to Rutaceae.

Aegle marmelos (wood apple) *Feronia asidissima or Feronia limonia* (Elephant apple), *Murraya exotica.*

The family Rutaceae spread over 140 genera and 1300 species (Lowrence), 120 genera and 1200 species (Engler), Willis (1966) included 150 genus and 900 species. Cronquist (1968), reported 1600 species in this family. However, in

India nearly 16 genera and 75 species are recorded. Bhattacharya and Dutta (1956) reported that about 78 species from Rutaceae family have their origin in India.

Citrus characters within species, represents high frequencies bud sport, interspecific and generic hybrid, caused inconveniance in classification. Among the classification Swingle and Tanaka classification are note worthy.

Citrus Classification

W.T. Swingle recognized 16 species under the genus citrus, whereas Tanaka (1954) described 144 species. Swingle's treatment was not sufficiently comprehensive and he considered most species to be of hybrid origin, rejected other than wild form and did not covered many Japanese, Chinese and Indian origin.

Swingle divided the genus citrus

Swingle classified citrus in two sub-genera, 16 species and 8 botanical varieties.

Citrus Genus
- Eucitrus (10 species)
- Papeda (6 species)

Eucitrus	*Papeda*
C. medica	*C. ichangensis*
C. aurantifolia	*C. micrantha*
C. aurantium	*C. latipes*
C. sinensis	*C. celebica*
C. reticulata	*C. macroptera*
C. grandis	*C. hystrix*
C. paradisii, C. indica	
C. tachibana	
C. limon	

Tanka (1954) was more comprehensive and detailed contained excessive number of species. Classified 2 sub-genera and 144 species.

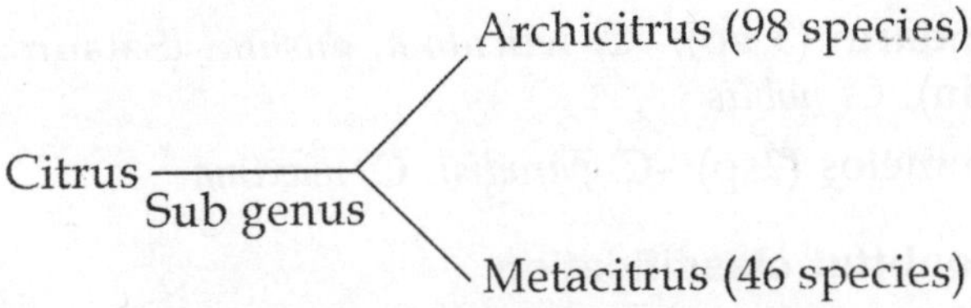

Genus Citrus (2 subgenera, 144 species)

Sub genera- Archicitrus (5 section, 98 secies)

Section 1- Papeda (12 sp)

2. Limonellus (16 sp)
3. Citrophorum (21 sp)
4. Aruntium (28 sp)
5. Cephalocitrus (21 sp)

Sub genus 2. Metocitrus

Section 1. Osmocitrus (9 sp)

2. Acrumen (36 sp)
3. Pseudofortunella (1sp)

Hogson Classification reported 159 species

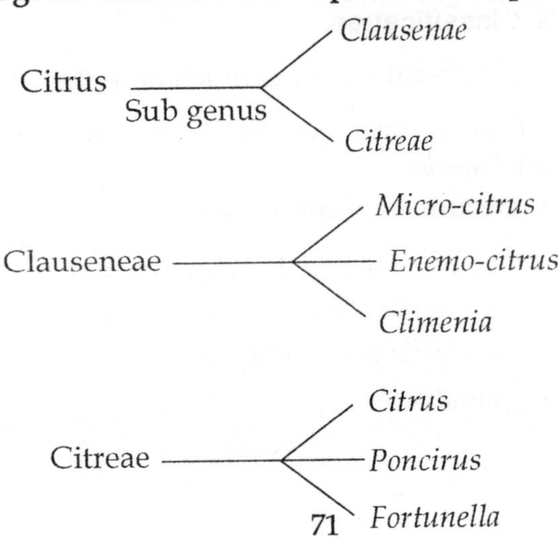

A. Acid member (6 sp)_C. *medica, limon, auranfolia, Jambhiri, Limetta. limettoide*

B. The orange (2 sp) C. *aurantium,* C. *sinensis*

C. Mandarin (3 sp). C. *reticulata, unshiu,* (Satsuma mandarin), C. *noblis*

D. Pummelos (2sp) –C. *paradisi,* C. *maxima*

Other doubtful classification

(1) C. *Limonia* (2) C. *bargamia* (3) C. *myrtifolia* (4) C. *madurensis*

Bhattacharya and Dutta, (1956)

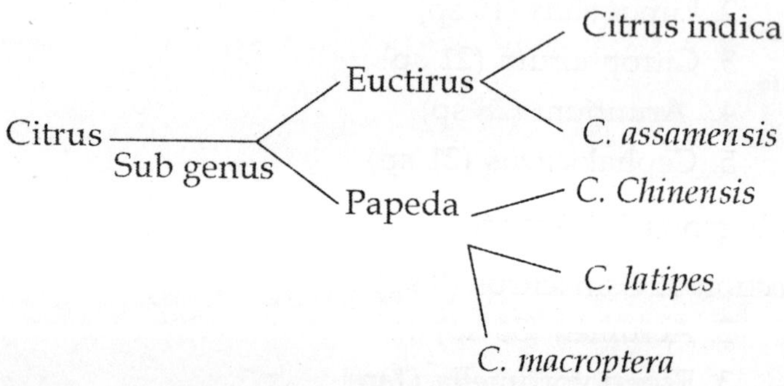

Swingle classification

Ranjit Singh's Classification

Ranjit Singh's classification is much accepted

Genus *Citrus* (2 sub genera) Subgenus-*Euctitrus* (8 sections) and *Papeda.*

(A) Section A. Decumana Group (7sp)

Species : 1. C. *pennivesiculata* (Gajanimma)

2. C. *pennivesiculata* var. assamensis

3. C. *sem[erflorens* (Sadaphal)

4. C. *paradisi*

5. C. *grandis*
6. C. *megaloxycarpa*
7. C. *meglaoxycarpa var. keem*

(B) **Medica Group** C. *medica,* C. *medica var. ethrog* (4sp) C. *medica var sacrodactylus* (finger citron) C. *limonimedica.*

(C) **Limonoid Group** (10 sp) *limon,* C. *karna,* C. *pseudolimon, limonia,* soh Jhalia, Acidless. C. *Jambhiri* (intermediate type), C. *Jambhiri* Katajamir type

(D) **Aurantium**, Group (5 sp) *Sinensis, aurantium* (bitter sweet orage) C. *aurantium* (proper sweet orange)

C. *aurantium* Var myrtifolia (Myrtale orange)

E. **Aurantoid Group** (3 species)

c. *regulosa,* (Indian Grape fruit)

Jenura tenga

C. *madaraspatana* (Kichili)

F - **Acrumen Group** (6 sp)

C. *noblis* (King mendarin), C. *unshiu* (Satsuma mandarin)

C. deliciosa, C. *retialate,* C. *reticulate* var austera

C. *lycopersicaeformis* (Cleopatra, Billi Kichili)

G- **Limonellus Group** (3 species)

C. *limettioides*

C. *limettioides* Var latifolia

C. *aurantifoila* (Acid lemon)

H. **Pseudofortunella group** (3 sp)

C. *indica* (Indian. Wild oranges)

C. *tachibana*

C. *madurensis*

Other : sub-genus Papeda

C. *ichangensis*

C. *latipes*

C. *micrantha*

C. *micrantha* var *microcarpa*

C. *hystrix*

C. *macroptera*

Modern System of Classification

This system of classification based on the quantity and properties of the certain organic biochemical compounds present in different parts of the plants. Smith 1976 first attempted this classification. It is purely controlled by genes, proved to be most accurate.

(A) Phenolic compound present in the plants parts : Divided into two groups -
  - (i) Simple phenolic compound in the ovule of flower
  - (ii) contain flavanoid compound

(B) On the basis of fatty acids present in the cell sap of xylem tissue -
  - (i) Palmitic acid - 36 species
  - (ii) Palmiticoleic acid - 12 species
  - (iii) Linoleic acid - 20 species
  - (iv) Linolenic acid - 21 species
  - (v) Oleic acid - 13 species

(C) Based on the enzymes present in the root hairs -
  - (i) As per the peroxidase activity of root hairs (4 group) and based on the polypenal activity of root hairs (3 groups)

(D) Based on the content of saturation of Carbon atoms present in alkaline compounds of the petals of flowers.

Salient features of genus *Citrus*

i) Plants are thorny with few exception, evergreen tree or shrubs.

ii) Leaves are compound, simple and persistent in nature thick leathery dotted with translucent oil cells, unfoliate, petiole winged Bisexual flowers, axillary, solitary or in cluster or small terminal cymes, petals scented, calyx small, cupped petal usually 5 stamens numerous (15-60) ovary compound, 8-16 celled, style deciduous.

iii) Fruits hesperidium, spherical or oblong in shape with lathery rind.

iv) Green when immature and yellow orange and red at maturity.

v) Abundant oil gland with albedo and flabedo interior of fruit divided in several segment by thin membrane wall, which are filled with juice vesicles.

vi) Seeds contain nuceller embryony.

vii) Hesperidium is a superior many celled fleshy fruit, develop from syncarpous pistil with axil placentation, endocarp projects inwards forming distinct chambers and the apocarps and mesocarp fused together to form the loose or tight skin rind called **albedo.**

Important *Citrus* Species

Poncirus trifaliata

The generic name of poncirus is changed to *Trifocitrus* (Surguladze, 1979). It is also known as trifoliate ovary, previously, it was under the genera *citrus trifoliata.* Central and Northern China is native home of trifoliate orange.

i Plant is deciduous in nature having trifoliate leaf with long sharp pointed spines.

ii It is most hardy plants used as root stock.

iii It is cold hardy plant, highly thorny. Flowers nearly sessile borne on one year old shoot, petal narrow and claw like at the base, stamens numerous free, ovary 6-8 celled.

iv pulp is acidic contains bitter oil, acrid oil which makes it inedible.

Fortunella (Kumquat):- A genus having few species out of which Fortunella

F. japonica, F. margarita, F. crassiflolia, F. hindsii are important.

i) Small bushy, shrub, evergreen, rarely of 10 feet height, densely branched, small spines.

ii) Leaf unifoliate smaller, simple, wingless, very small petiole. Plant thorn less, ornamental.

iii) Flowers white, smaller, solitary or in branches in leaf axils either on current season flesh or last season growth pedicels bracted with one or two smaller bracts 4-5 petals, stamens 16-20 with 2 ovules in each cell, stigma caitate, fruit small oblong or globose, rind thin sweet and edible.

iv) Fruit orange colour, very thick sweet edible rind.

v) Mild acid pulp, juicy, seed cotyledons is green harder to cold than any *Citrus* species.

vi) Fruits are mainly used for candy and marmeled preparation.

Citron (*C. medica* Linn)

Real citron grows in Garo hills of Assam, Weight (1840-50) reports that citron has been found to grow wild in Niligri Hills *C. limon* (Lin.) Burmann earlier name *C. medica* var Limon, Linu *C. limoi* (lin) Burmann *Limon vulgaris* Mill *C limonium* (Vulgaris).

C. assamensis - It is a new species, the aroma of the rind gives typical zinger small. Original speciemen has been sent to Kew Herbarium for identification.

***Citrus mitis* (Hazara)**

Previously considered as Kumquat now it is hybrid of *Citrus X Fortumella*,

Smallest fruit of ornamental type. *Citrus microcarpa* is oldest name available name for the taxon *Citrus mitis* originally adopted as the basionym for X *citrofortunella mitis* (Calamondin), hence, new combination X *Citrofortunella* microcarpa is necessary (Wijnands, 1984).

C. jambhiri (Rough Lemon)- Called jambhiri in U.P, Jattikhatti in Punjab and Sohmouty in Assam.

i) Trees are vigorus, large upright spreading with thorny.
ii) Leaves medium, light green in colour and serration of leaf margin are not sharp.
iii) Smaller flower mandarin like purple tinged, produced almost throughout the year namely in spring and late summer.
iv) Fruit differ distinctly with lemon by having round to sub globose shape with cavity or depression surrounding the apical papilla or nipple, nipple surrounding by deep irregular areolar furrow with rough fruit skin.
v) Flesh yellow core open at maturity.
vi) It is highly polyembroyonic species of Indian Origin.
vii) It is most important citrus root stock of world.

C. aurantium (bitter or sour orange or sevella orange).

i) It is highly polyembryonic and cold hardy species tree just like sweet orange.
ii) Tree upright thorny medium sized, dark green distinctly scented leaves.
iii) Survive well in unfavourable condition like frost, excess moisture and neglected land and resistant gummosis.
iv) Flowers are large and sweet scented.
v) Fruit very sour and bitter, fruit medium sized, orange red skinned at maturity, central core semi-hollow rind separates easily, highly seeded.
vi) Leaf is simple but broadly winged petiole.
vii) Flowers are used for perfuming industry (oil of neroli).

Sweet Orange (*Citrus sinensis*) (Linn) Osbeck, origin Southern China or Indo-China, earlier it was called *C. aurantium var* sinensis Linnaeus (in **Species Plantrum**, 1783, 1753). Loureiro (1790) designated the sweet orange as C.

aurantium, while Osbeck (1775) segregated it from sour orange as different species and named *C.sinensis (*Linn) Osbeck).

1. A highly polyembronic species of Chinese origin.
2. Trees are vigorous, long and somewhat thorny.
3. Leaf apex blunt pointed, narrowly winged petiole.
4. Fruit subglobose to oval in shape, orange coloured light skinned with solid central core.
5. Tree pendulous and evergreen.
6. Sweet juicy flavour, seeds are few to many.
7. Segments are tightly arranged to one another.

Cultivars

Malta Blood Red, Masambi (popular in Andhra Pradesh, Gujrat and Maharashtra), Sathgudi (originated in Sathgur (T.N.), Valenica, Pineapple, Washington Navel Orange (having a rudimentary secondary fruit emboded in the fruit apex, Shamouti of Israel (famous for seedlessness), Succari of Egypt, Dobla Fina from Spain, Joffa, Valencia Late, Hamlin.

Yuvraj Blood Red

It is a clonal selection from sweet orange early and seedless.

Cleopatera mandarin (C. *reshini* Tanaka) also known as Chota, or Billi Kichili in India and cleopatera in USA.

1. It is attractive ornamental tree, bear through out the year.
2. Tree are attractive round top, symmetrical and thorn less with small dark green leaves.
3. Fruit is orange red, small, highly depressed at apex.
4. Rind thin, texture soft and juicy.
5. Seeds small and polyembryonic.

***C. paradisii* Macf**

Grape fruit or Chakotra or Mithora). As per revised taxonomic system and Vavilov Institute of Plant Industry (VIR) section *Cephalocitrus* is divided into 2 species. C *grandis* and C. *paradisi* (Karaya, 1987). However, isozyme, protiens and sabinene content in leaf oil, browing reaction of cut tissue and peiole and pollen structure it is concluded that C. *grandis* is female parent and C. *sinensis* is male of C. *paradisi* (Scora *et al*. 1982). C. *grandis* (Linn) Osbeck Origin - Polynesia and Malay (Hooker 1872, Brandis 1890 Webber, 1946 and many others).

Sour Pummelos (C. *megaloxycarpa* Lushington), very big size, intensely acid fruit.

i) The trees are large round top with dense foliage twigs are angular or round.

ii) Leaves are longer than sweet orange but comparatively narrowed and smaller than pummelo.

iii) Flowers are large and borne single or in cluster.

iv) Fruits are longer than sweet orange but smaller than pammelo.

v) Fruits are generally globose or pear shaped having white or pink juice rind surface yellow colour.

vi) Seeds are smaller or compared to pummelo.

vii) Cultivars Foster, Ruby, Marsh, Duncan (seedless), Thompson, Ganganagar, Saharnpur, Marsh Seedless, Foster seedless, Saharanpur Pink, Triumph.

Trifoliate Orange *(Poncirus trifoliata or Trifocitrus)* (Surguladze, 1979).

i) It is inedible and remarkably different from oranges.

ii) Trees are deciduous in nature, with large straight spines.

iii) Small compound leaf with winged petiole.

iv) Flower buds are small single, lateral protected by small fleshy scale.

v) Flowers are small, petals are fine, white in colour papery type, stamens are numerous ovary have 6-8 locules.
vi) Rind is thick, numerous droplets of aerole oil gland, highly unpleasant taste, fruits fall down after ripening.

Sweet Lime (*C. limetloides*):- It is highly polyembryonic species, originated in India, sweet lime is classified from old lime because of its non acidic sweet juice, it is commercially grown in Egypt, as root stock.

i) Trees are large and spreading type.
ii) Leaves of same size at those of sweet orange, leaf lamina characteristically cuped (about rolled).
iii) Fruit is bigger than acid lime and flowers are large and white fruits are flobose to ellipsoid in shape.
iv) Staminioides flowers are more than the pistilate and complete hence fruit sciting is very poor.
v) There is no descript type of cultivars only Mitha Nimbu and Sharbati of India belongs to this species.

Rangpur Lime (*C. limonia* or Canton lemon):- pollen morphology study indicates that pollen grain of Canton lemon were very different from mandarin (Ye-Yin *et al.*, 1982).

i) Plants are very vigorous, medium size spreading and drooping habit.
ii) Small thorns are present.
iii) Foliage dull green just like to mandarin.
iv) New plant growth is slightly purple tinged, flower are of small size like mandarian but buds and petals are deeply tinged.
v) Fruits are small in size often with short nipple, rind yellow to raddish orange thin and moderately loose.
vi) Segments 8-10 loosely adherent axis large and hollow at maturity numerous seeds. Fruit retain on tree for long time.

Karna Khatta (*C. karna*):- It is also known as Sohsarkar.

i) Tree medium to large somewhat similar to that of rough lemon leaves large with sirulate margin and winged petiole. Young shoot thorny.

ii) Flowers large and pigmented (purple tinged).

iii) Fruits medium rind surface irregular and apical papilla well developed rind, thick moderately 9-13 segments, medium to short axis, solid to spongy. Seeds many 20-30, cotyledons white.

Citrus Jambhiri

Citrus limon

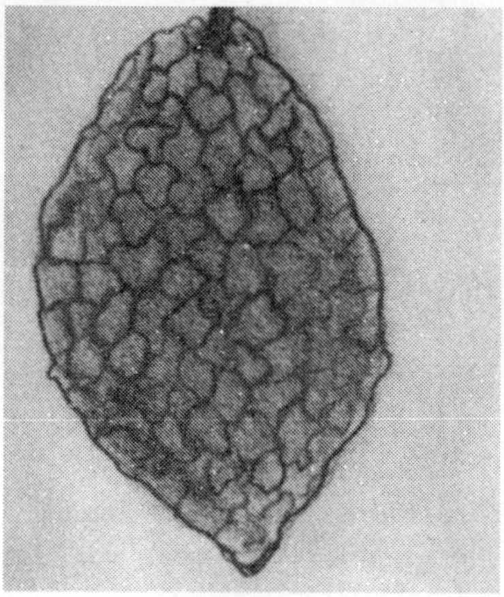

Citrus limon

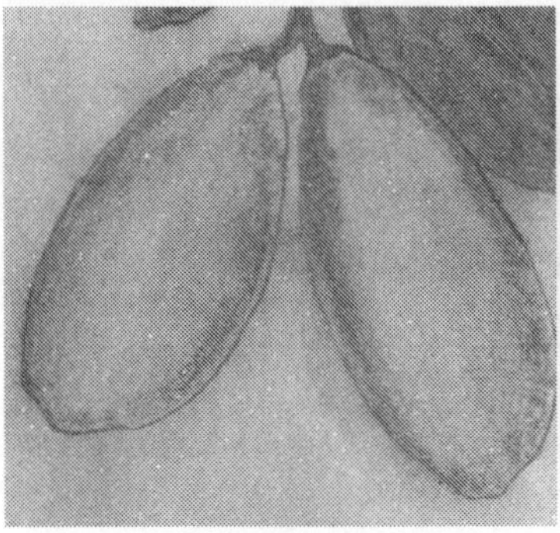

Citrus limon

Citrus nobilis

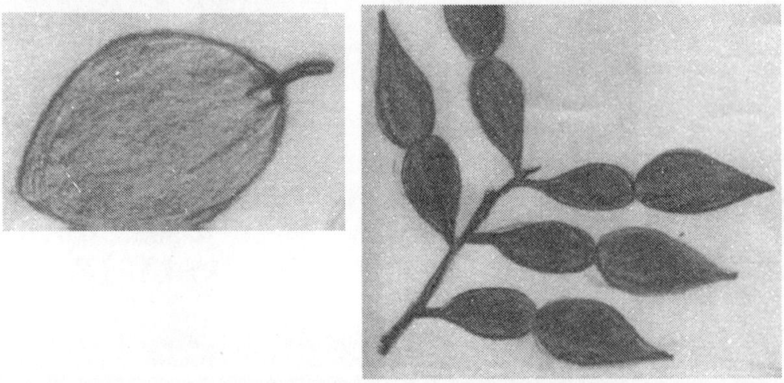

Leaves & fruit of *Citrus ichangenesis*

Citrus karna

Citrus jambhiri

(Photo Curtesy Mr. Bilal Ahmad)

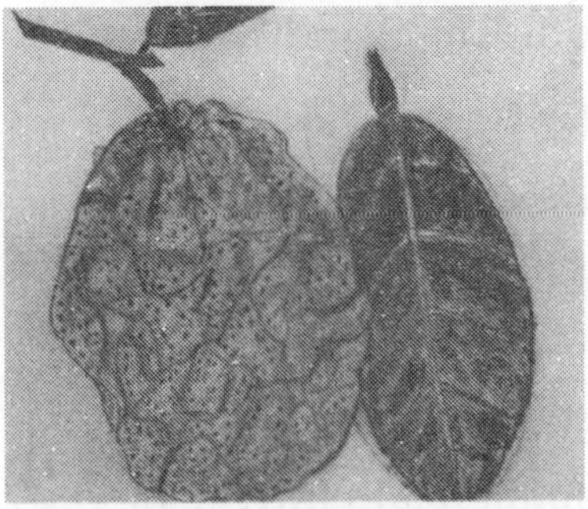

Citrus megaloxycarpa

Mandarin

(*C. reticulata*):- It is called Tangarin in USA and Santra in India, highly poly embroyonic species.

i) Medium size upright tree growth (cylindrical), bushy, evergreen, erector semi erect in spreading, lanceolate leaves, petiole are short almost wingless.

ii) Small white perfect flower.

iii) Fruit medium sized globose, sweet in taste ring loose, easily separable from fruit, core open at maturity.

iv) Rind colour scarlet orange when fully ripe, pulp juicy, juice sub acidic, 10-14 Segments in each fruits, seeds pointed with light green cotyledons.

v) Centre of pulp is widely hollow.

Nagpur, Coorg Orange (Coorg and Chickmangalur) **Satsuma-** Best mandarins of world commonly grown in Japan, other species of Satsuma group is Mikado, Ikeda, Owari, Sileverhill and Wase. Fruits are seedless.

Kinnow mandarin Kinnow first generation hybrid between King Orange X Willow leaf by H.B. Frost at California Experiment Station in 1915. (*C. nobilis X C. deliciosa*) popular in Punjab, it is most sucessful introduction.

Khasi Mandarin (north-eastern region)

Darjeeling and Sikkim mandarin.

Ponkan (South China and Farmosa).

Mudkhed Seedless

It is mutant of Nagpur Mandarin and seedless in nature.

Clementine (Algeria) monoembryonic and early maturing cultivar.

Beauty- most popular in Australia

Dancy – Commercial cultivar of USA excellent fruit quality.

Acid Lime (*C. aurantifolia*) or sour lime

It is a highly polyembryonic distinctive species of great commercial importance.

1. Tree small, bushy with small but sharp spines.
2. Leaves are small with narrowly winged petiole.
3. Flowers and fruit small, fruit round to oval, mature irregularly throughout year thin slanned, greenish yellow colour fruit.

Sai sarbati

It was evolved from Mahatma Phule Krishi Vidyapeeth, Rahuri. It is high yielder suitable for summer cropping tolerant to Canker and tristeza.

Seedless Lime

Fruits are oblong in shape, thin skin, late and prolific bearer.

Jai Devi

It was developed from Fruit Research Station, Periakulum, high yielding, juicy, thin peel and pleasant aroma.

Chakardhar

It is seedless and thornless selection in Kagazilime.

Tahiti Lime (*C. latifolia*)

It is large fruited acid lime. Plants are large spreading and thornless, cold resistant. Fruits are large in size, seedless, late maturing triploid and produce non-viable pollen. It is considered hybrid between lime and lemon.

West Indian Lime

Commercially grown in Mexico, Florida, West Indies, India and Kagazi ilime in India.

Baramasi Lemon

Pramalini, Parbhani and Vikram

Fruits are borne in cluster clonally selected at MAU, Parbhani, Maharastra.

PKM-1 evolved at Periyakulam clonally, heavy bearer tree.

Florida, in India mainly grown in southern region, fruit normally seedless.

Hybrid-2, Hybrid-4 and N.52 are found to be resistant to Citrus canker.

Lemon Barmasi (*C. Limon*)

Trees are medium sized spreading new flushes are pigmented leaf margin sub-serrated petiole medium sized narrowly winged.

1. Flower bud pigmented, pistil densely dotted with oil gland.
2. Fruit oval to elliptic with pointed nipple, fruit light yellow colour, core solid, juice in ample amount lemon oil most important citrus.

Cultivars

- Eureka and Libson (USA)
- Femminello and Monachello (Italy)
- Malta Lemon (Bushy, compact, very dwarf tree)
- Mayeri Lemon
- Nepali oblong
- Kagazi Kalan
- Italian Round
- Assam Lemon
- Bhadri Lemon (Biggest lemon)
- Pant Lemon.
- Hill Lemon (Galgal) *C. pseudolimon*

Pummelo or Shaddock

(*C. grandis* (L) Osbeck):- It is also called *C. maxima,* however, Scora and Nicklson (1986), advised that *C. maxima* is the correct name on the basis of historical priority under the ICBN rule.

i) Spreading round topped almost thorn less tree, leaves large with broadly winged petiole, lower surface of leaf vein pubescence.
ii) flower, very large crowded in short axillary racemes.
iii) Fruit large sized subglobse to pyriform thick and spongy rind, fruit sweet and moderately juicy.
iv) Seed very large coarsely veined.
v) Two type of fruits white fleshed and red or pink fleshed.

Citrus grandis cultivar Nagpur (Chakotra)

Major Citrus group

Mandarin Group

Citrus reticulata

C. unshiu

C. *deliciosa*

C. *noblis*

C. *reshmi* (spice mandarin)

C *medurensis* (Calamondin)

C. *madaras patina*

C. *tangerine* (Dancytangarin)

Orange Group

C. *sinensis*

C. *aurantium*

3. Pummelo or grape fruit group

C. *grandsis or* C. *maxima*

C. *paradisii*

4. Acid Group

C. *liman*

C. *jambhiri*

C. *aurantifolia*

C. *limettoides*

C. *medica L. (Citron)* C. *medica* Var. Muliensis

It is found in Mulizang, large fruit (1360- 2378 g.) are ridged and are monoembryonic, the juice is acidic and fruit has medicinal uses. Mulicitron is variety of C *medica* (Wang et al 1983). Cultivars belong to C *medica* was investigated cytotaxonomically, it seems that sour Citron or sweet citron are taxonomically very close to each other (Borger, 1978).

C. *karma*

C. *latifolia* (Persian lemon)

C. *Limetta* (*Pani Jamir* of Assam)

C. *limonia* (Rangpur lime)

Wild and Semi Wild species of Citrus

C. *indica* (Indian wild orange)

C. *latipes* (khasi Papeda)

C. *macroptera (*Melanesia papeda)

C. *assamensis*.

Other related genera of Rutaceae

Pancirus trifoliata

Fortunella

Intergeneric hybrids.

Citrange- *Poncirus trifoliata x C sinesis*

Citramgequat- *Poncirus trifoliata x fortunella*

Citrangedin- *Citrange x C. sinesis.*

Citrange – *Citrange x poncirus.*

Citrumelo- *Poncirus x Paradisi*

Citrandarin- *Poncirus x reticulate*

Citremon- *Poncirus x C. limon.*

Citradia- *Poncirus x C aurantima.*

Citrumquat- *Poncirus x fortunella japonica or margaridta* (very difficult hybrid to Breed)

Procimequat- *F .Japonica x C. aurantifolia* cv mexicon X *F hindisii.*

Limequat- *C. aurantifolia X F. Japonica.*

Orangequat- *C reticulata* var Satsuma *X F. Japonica X F. margarita* cv Meiwa.

Tangor- *C. reticulata C. Sinesis*- important cultivars are Temple, Clemntine, Monreal, Umatilla.

Tangelo- *C. reticulata X C. paradisi* cultivars Orlando, Sampson, Minneola, Seminole.

Lemonime- Lemonx lime- Cultivar Parrine.

Lemonage- *C. limon X C. sinesis*

Lemandarin- *C. limon X C. reticulate.*

C. lapiniji (C. clementina X *C. delliosa*). The species is self-sterile, does not cross with its parent. Highly frost resistant and large fruit. (Kapanadze, 1985)

- Chemical taxonomy of the genus Citrus, lemon appear to have trihybrid origin and lime also have complex hybrid (Scora, 1983).
- *C. halimii-* is between the genera *Citrus* and *Fortunella,* ovary morphology indicates (Scora, 1983).
- A study of the collection of Japanese, Chinese Yuzu Oranges at the VIR Experimental Station of Sukhumi, Gerogian, resulted 5 new taxa of Junos type in *Citrus* genus. *C Juko, C serotina, C. kinosu, C. sechen and C. tanaka* and one new sub species *C. Juko sub species* sjanchen (Kokaya, 1983).

Citrus Biodiversity in India

The north east hilly region is considered as a centre of origin of mandarin and few other citrus species, sixteen species of citrus, 52 verities and seven natural hybrid of Assam were described by Bhattacharya and Dutta as early as in 1956. They also reported two species of sub genus Eucitrus viz *C. indica, C assamensis,* and three species of sub genus of Papeda viz; *C. ichangensis, C. latipes,* and *C. microptera* which grow at high altitude. *Citrus indica,* considered to be the most primitive species probably originator of cultivated type citrus. It is found in various fruit form in N.E. region. Different forms of Pummelo, adajamir, sweet lime etc is found in this region. Mandarin orange is concentrated in Maharastra (Nagpur, Amravathi, Wardha, and Yavatmal). NE region (Assam, Arunanchal Pradesh, Meghalaya, Karnataka (Kodager) T.N. (Nilgris, Palani, Shevroyhills) Kerala (Wynad), Sathpura hills of M.P area adjoining Vidharbha region of M.P. Kinnow orange, spread in N.W. India (Punjab, part of H.P), U.P., Rajasthan, sweet orange are adopted in arid tropics to

subtropics, (A.P, Maharashtra, Punjab, part of T.N, Raj, U.P). In A.P, Sathgudi, in Western and Central India Mosambi in N.W. India Malta, Jaffa, and Valencia are popular. Acid lime grown on large scale in T.N, A.P, Maharastra, Karnataka States, Assam lemon is popular in North East region of India.
C. *karna* Rafinesque Soh- sarkar or son arsarkar of Khasi hills.
C. *limetta* (Risso) Lushington (Grows wild in Nilgris Hills)
C. *reticulate Blanco Narangi (C. reticulate)* C. *nobilis* Loureiro

Indian Wild Orange C. *indica,* Tanaka was first who identified I.W. Orange at Nowgong distt of Khasi Hills, Manipur in Assam, 3-6 feet height, zigzag branching, young branches terete, glabrous and spiroum, leaf wing less apex caudate, veins prominent flower solitary male and female 22-25 filament joint forming tube, fruit spherical to depressed globose, sub-pyriform small deep orange, 8-11 segment.

Holong- Tenga C *megalory* mark peculiar roughness of rind.

Chapter **6**

Systematic Description of Banana

Banana, Apple of paradise is one of the fourth most important food crop in terms of gross value exceeded only paddy, Wheat, milk products. Raising its International importance resulted formulation of International Network for Improvement of Banana Plantain (INIBP) plays vital role in the global partnership. Banana is rich in vitamins. Owing to its multifaceted uses and high economic returns, it is referred as Kalpatharu (A plant of virtue). An ample amount of diversity occur throughout the world, in this chapter its systematic position is being delt.

Classification

Division - Phanerogams

Sub division - Angiospermae

Class - Monocotyledones

Order - Zingiberales

Families- Musaceae, Strelitziaceae, Lowiaceae, Zingiberaceae, Cannaceae, Merantaceae.

Characteristics feature of order Zingiberales

1. Plants are herbaceous with rhizomes and fibrus roots, stem often very short, formed by imbricate leaf sheath, leaves spirally arranged, sheath open or rarely closed.
2. Calyx and Corolla in separate whorls, stamens 5-6 or reduced to one, rest transformed into petaloid staminodes. Ovary inferior, fruit capsule or fleshy indehiscent.

3. Distributed in tropical, sub-tropical or in humid regions.

Systematic position of Musaceae family as per taxonomist

Hutchinson	Bentham and Hooker
Angiospermae (Phylum)	Angiospermae (Group)
Monocotyledons (S.phlum)	Monocotyledonae (S group)
Calyciferae (Division)	Epigynae (series)
Musaceae (Family)	Musaceae (family)

Engler and Prantle

Angiospermae

Monocotyledones (Class)

Scitamineae (Order)

Musaceae (Family)

Salient feature of Musaceae

1. Plant generally perennial in nature, tree like, giant herbs, stem stout, unbranched stem, pseudo stem.
2. Leaves and bract spirally arranged, leaf large, alternate simple, entire leaf, abundant amount of watery sap present in petiole. Leaves exceptionally large.
3. Flower unisexual, calyx tubular, split down one side, stamens 5-6 free anther 2-locular.
4. Fruit indehiscent in nature. According to Hutchinson include a single genus *Musa* with about 45 species.
5. Gynoecium, tricarpellary, syncarpous with inferior trilocular ovary, axile placentation.
6. Flower mostly unisexual, clustered and enclosed by large coloured spathaceous bract male flower borne towards upper bract, female within lower bract.

Musa Species

1. Banana is vigorous herbs, real stem is rhizome on which

large number of buds or eyes develops, found under ground, above ground stem is pseudostem.

2. Leaves are broad with parallel venation.
3. Inflorescence primordial initiated from heart of pseudostem.
4. Desert Banana - *Musa paradisiaca*
5. Plantain or vegetable banana- *M. sapientum.*
6. Fibre banana (Manila hemp) *M. textiles.*
7. Ornamentel type of banana (Bird of paradise)

   M niginae, *M basjoo*, *M. superba*, *M. ensete* etc.

There are two genera viz *Ensete* and *Musa* with about 50 species.

Ensete - old and declining genus originated in Asia and spread to Africa. It has about 6-7 species *Ensete ventricosa* is reported to be grown in Ethiopia as food Crop.

Musa - Genus divided into 5 sections.

Section 1

Eumusa- (2 n=22, 33, 44):- It is largest section with 13-15 species; distributed in India, pseudostem exceeds the height of 3m, bract dull in colour. It comprise wild species and cultivated type Eumusa contain all edible species except *M. fehi* *M. acuminate* (seeded inedible type ssp *burmannica*, ssp, *siameae*, ssp. *malaccensis*., ssp. *truncate*, ssp. *microcarpa*, ssp. *banksi*, ssp. *errans*, ssp. *zebrine*, all AA genome), *M. bulbisiana* (*M. schizocarpa*, *M. basjoo*, *M. cheesmani*, *M. flaviflora* *M. halabanensis*, *M. itinerans*, *M. nagensium*, *M. sikkimensis*, *M. sumatra* (all B btype genome). Inflorescence pedent to semi-pedent.

Section 2

Rhodochlayms (2n=22) 5-7 species are found from India to Indonesia. Pseudostem less than 3m, inflorescence erect with only few bract, no parthenocarpy, important species are *M. mannii, M. aurantiaca, M. rosacea, M. rasea, M. rubra, M. laterita, M. ornate, M.sanguinea, M velutina,* two species *M. ornate* and *M. velutina* grows as ornamental plant.

Section 3

Australimusa- (2n =20) occurred from Queensland to Philippines, inflorescence pedent, semipedent as well as erect. It comprise two type i) wild species, ii) cultivar fei type (Eaten in Polynesian Island after cooking, fruits are generally parthencarpic and predominantly female sterile), fruiting bunch straight and contain red sap. Flesh yellow, skin orange colour after ripening. In fei type *M. maclayi, M. boman, M. lolodensis, M. peekalie, M. textilis, M. jackeyi* comprise.

Section 4

Callimusa- (2n = 20) it comprise species viz *M. beccarii, M. borneesis, M. violescens, M. coccinea, M. gracilis-* psedostem 1.5 height, fruit oblong, orange yellow black, cylindrical seeds. Mainly used as ornamental purpose.

Section 5

Incertae sedis- (2n = 14) - This group include *M. ingens,* which unearthed from New Guinea grows to a height of over 10 m and in the largest herb known.

Description of some important Musa species

Musa bulbisiana: - Mostly seeded diploid, found in Chittagaon, plant green or yellowish green. Pseudostem 6m height and 30 cm in diameter at base, leaf wide oblong, rachis, 20 male flowers per bractrs pulp. Black and minute seed blotches, slight or absent on pseudo stem.

M. accuminata

Pseudostem 3-6, usually having blotched with brown or black leaf sheath and petiole often covered with bloom rachis and peduncle thickly, fingers prominently beaked, bract apex acute, short pedicel, pulp whitish or yellowish in colour asymmetrical found in Assam and Burma.

M. nagensium

It is most widely distributed in all seven North-Eastern states. Due to its conspicuously black pseudostem, it get confused from *M. balbisiana* by amateurs, very tall plant, maroon, shiny male bud, 8-15 hands, self pollinated, highly female fertile with 80-100 big, shiny and warty seeds, orange flesh, very sweet (32°B). Male bud fascination and multiple male buds in a bunch are often noticed in this species.

M. itinerans

It has rhizomatious stem, buds crawl away from mother plants and emerged at 1-1.5 m distance, hence referred as walking banana. Highly drought tolerant, owing to its dormant rhizomatous stem, conspicuous violet pigmentation in juvenile phase, 4-6 hands, stocky short beaked fruits, 150 seeds/fruit.

M. paradisiaca

Jacob made comprehensive studies of banana clones and observed that use of *M. paradisiaca* is restrictive and proposed new species *M sapidiaca* in view of its hybrid origin (*M. accuminata* X *M. bulbisiana*). Jacob considered *M. sapientum* is synonyms of some species belonging *M. paradisiacal* subsequently, Linnaeus binomials *M. sapientum* and *M. paradisiaca* abandoned and described utilizing cytotaxonomy according to the system *M. accuminata*. Colla was used to describe pure seedless (AA, AAA forms). *M.bullisiona* Colla was applied to pure *bulbisiana* cultivars having AB, ABB, AAB genome.

Simmonds and Shepherd (1955) developed the technique for indicating the relative contribution of two wild species for constitution of any cultivar through a scoring technique of certain morphological character and applying the derived information for distinguishing *M. accuminata* type from those of *M. bulbisiana*. Number one given for each character in which *accummata* agrees for each characters from *M bulbisiana* the score 5 was given and intermediate expressions of the characters was give score of 2, 3 or 4 as per intensity of characters. A cultivar derived from *M. balbisiana* have a large score from *M. accuminata*, small score viz. AA (15-23); AAA- (15-23); AAB (24-26) AB (49) ABB (59-63); ABBB (67). Simmonds and Shepherd (1955), Stover and Simmonds (1987), proposed revised classification of edible banana, AA/AAA (15-25); AAA (26-46); ABB (59-63); ABBB (61-69); BB /BBB (70-75); score described.

Banana diversity

The edible banana is believed to have originated from hot tropical regions of South-East Asia. (Spiden, 1926; Sauer, 1952) extending from India to Paupa, New Guinea including Malaysia and Indonesia.

India is the second largest diversity of indigenous banana in the world. 600 types of Musa germplasms are found world over and 300 germplasm found in India alone. It could be assumed that the fruit has evolved with the civilization and found in India valley as early as 327 B.C. *M. accuminata* found region of India viz. Assam, Arunachal Pradesh, Tripura and Mizorm lie at the point where *M. accuminata* (South East Asia) both wild species inter mingled and developed large number of germplasm. Wild species found in the part of India include *M. accuminata, M. chinensis, M. textiles, M. bulbisiana,* several species from the section Rhodochlamys (*M. oranta*) is chiefly represented in Assam, Myanmar and Thailand and *Ensets glaucum* also found in India. Edible banana is native to old word particularly south - east - Asia (Simmonds, 1962), Malaya is primary centre of origin of M. acuminate.

Important cultivars of Banana

AB- Chinichampa (Neypoovan), Najali Poovan, Sofedvelchi.

AAA-Dwarf Cavendish, Robusta, Thellochakkarakeli, Jahaji, Borjahaji, Robusta, Dwarf Cavendish, Honda, Grand Naine, Sindhurni, Hanuman, Ardhapuri, Amritsagar, Giant Governor, Lacatan.

AAB- Amrithpani (Silk), Karpurachakkarakeli, ChiniChampa, Jatikol, Dig-Jowa (silk), Kulpait (silk) Malbhog, Poovan, Nendran (Plantain), Rasthali, Virupakshi, Pachanadan, Mortpan, Champa.

ABB- Monthan, Manohar, Kanchkol, Muthia, Kothia, Pisang Awak, Karpuravalli (Pisang Awak)

AAAA- Bodles Altafort

ABBB- Klue Tiparot.

Dwarf Covendish

(Synonyms- Basrai, Bhusawal, Vamanakeli, Giant Governor, Canary Banana). It is most important cultivar of India, plant dwarf, large fruit and curved, skin thick and greenish even after ripening but ripening during winter develop yellow colour, poor keeping quality, cultivar suitable for windy area and high density plantation.

Robusta

(Harichhal, Bombay Green) - True Robusta is not under cultivation in India except some semi tall to dwarf mutant. Fruit large, skin thick, greenish to dull yellow, sweet and delicious. It has some important mutants viz. Tall Monsmari (Australia), Poyo (W.Indies), Valery (Latin America) and Americani.

Lacatan

(Pisang Masak Hijau), Monte, Gisto, Giant Fig) - It is tall type cultivar.

Gross Michel

High gate and Cocos are two mutants. It was leading banana trade till 1950, but its susceptibility to Panama wilt, replaced the commercial status.

Red Banana

(Syn- Lal Velchi, Lalkela, Anupam, Agniswar, Rathambala etc). The cultivar, grown throughout world, pseudostem petiole, midrib and fruit peel in purplish red. The fruit is of good size and has characteristics aroma. It survive well in humid tropics and at higher altitude. It has highly susceptibility to bunchy top, fusarium wilt and nematode.

Rasthali

(AAB) Syn Amrithpani, Mortaman, Muthali, Malbhog, Silk fig, Apple, Pisang Rasthli). It is most popular choicest table type cultivar of West Bengal, Tamil Nadu, Karnataka, Andhra Pradesh, Kerala and Bihar. Plant tall, yellowish green stem with brownish blotches, raddish margin of petiole and leaf sheath. Fruit medium size resembled to Poovan in appearance, thin skin flesh firm, sweet with pleasant aroma. Longer crop duration and easy fruit dropping is drawbacks.

Poovan (AAB)

Plant tall hardy, grows vigorusly under ratooning system of cultivation. It is true cosmopolitan cultivars grows with similar vigour in India and West Indies. Typical feature is rose pink colour on the outer side of midrib, can be grown in marginal condition.

Virupakshi or Hill Banana (AAB)

Importantly grown in South India, it is tall strong and sturdy plant, fruits are thick skinned, turn yellowish green when ripe with distinctive flavour. It can be grown up to 2000 m avove sea level. Virupakhii is shy yielding cultivar Sirumalai Vannan; Kaali are ecotype of this cultivate.

Nendran (AAB)

French Plantain, Rajeli, Bharot, Kochi Kehel, Plantain) - It is dual purpose cultivar of Kerala, it has good keeping quality, bunch is not compact. This is best variety for chips industry. Nendran has 12-ecotype viz. Attu Nendran, Nava Nendran, Nedu Nendran, Myndoli, Quintal Mendran, Velethan, Otta Moongil, Chengali Kodan.

H-1 (Agniswar X Pisang lilin)

It has short cropping cycle, resistant to leaf spot, *Fusarium* wilt. It was evolved by Kerala Agricultural University Kannara. Average weight of bunch is 14-16 kg.

Co1 (Kadali X Kollar Laden) x *M. Bulbisiana* clone Sawai)

It was evolved by Tamil Nadu Agricultural University Coimbotore. Characteristically possess typical apple flavour of Virupakshi even when grown in plain.

Udayam (AAB)

It is heavy yielder (75.8 tonns/ha), high T.S.S 32 Brix, acid sweet taste. A single plant selection of Pisang Awak (ABB), good for windy area.

Chapter 7

Systematic Description of Grape

Grape is most important crop of sub tropical region. It has many uses and berries are very delicious. Almost all part of country produce grape. There are great confusion in its systematic position and taxonomy. India is also a centre of great diversity. The various aspect of grape taxonomy is being discussed in this chapter.

Classification

Division- Phanerogams

Sub- Division- Angiospermae

Class - Dicotyledons

Order- Rhamnales

Families- Vitaceae, Heterophyxidaceae, Elalagnaceae, Rhamnaceae,

Systematic position as per taxonomist classification

Bentham and Hooker	Hutchinson
Angiosperme (Group)	Angiospermae (Phylum)
Dicotyledons (Sub group)	Dicotyledones (S. phylum)
Polypetalae (Division)	Lignosae (Division)
Celastrales (order)	Rhamnales (order)
Ampelideae (family)	Vitaceae (family)
Engler and Prantle	
Angiospermae	
Dicotyledoneae (Class)	
Archichlamydeae (S.Class)	
Rhamnales (order)	
Vitaceae (family)	

Salient feature of Rhamnales Order

1. Tree, shrubs or climbers.
2. Leaves alternate or opposite simple to compound stipulate. Flower with stamens opposite to the petals or alternate with sepals. Petals imbricate or valvate, rarely absent seeds with copious or scanty endosperm present sometimes ruminate, embryo usually straight.

Characteristics feature of Vitaceae Family

Family Vitacea include 12 genera (Olmo, 1976) and 600 species The important genera *Vitis, Ampellocissus, Parthenocissus, Cissus, Tetrastigma, Cayratia, Leea.*

1. Mostly climbing type plant grown in tropical sub tropical and temperate region, plants climbing by means of tendrils.
2. Flower polygamous deciduous that is some individuals perfect and fertile and others imperfect with at most only a rudimentary ovary.
3. Stamens normally 5 or more.
4. Berry pulpy, seeded or seedless, fruit two loculed fleshy berry.

Salient features of genus *Vitis*

1. All the plants of this genus are woody, deciduous vines, climbing by tendril developed from terminal buds.
2. This genus has three types of flower i.e. male, female and hermaphrodite, *Vitis* species had been originally dioecious and sub-dioecious, but later on transformed to hermaphrodite (Olmo, 1976). *Vitis rotundifolia* is dioecious nature.
3. Inflorescence borne are cyme, opposite of a leaf at the node and bears large number of minute flowers bisexual or sometimes unisexual.
4. Fruit two loculed fleshy, seeds pyriform with beak like base (Caruncle).

5. genus *Vitis* is sub divided into two sub genus
   i) *Muscadinia*- It consists 3 species *M. Munsoniona, M. rotundifolia, M. popenoei* do not hybridize with *Euvitis* .Vitis genus was divided in two sub genus earlier, but now *Muscadinia* has been given generic status (Olmo, 1976).
   ii) *Euvitis* sub genus- De Lattin (1939) grouped many species of Euvities in the 9 sections given below. 1. Labruscae 2. Cinerascentes 3. Ripariae 4. Muscadinia 5. Aestivales 6. Rupestres 7. Incertae 8. Vinifera 9. Labruscoides.

As per report, all the authorities include the true grapes in the genus *Vitis* (it include 60 species).

Vitis species: - has been grouped as follows:

Family Vitaceae contain 10 genera (Rehder, 1958); 11 genera (Janick and Moore, 1977) and 12 genera (Olmo, 1976).

Section 1- ***Muscadinia-*** *Muscadinia* grape can be identified by tight bark that does not shed, unforked tendril and nodes without diaphragm (continuous pith at node), tendril intermittent, simple flower cluster, small seeds without beak, berries very large skin thick and tough.

i) *M . routundifolia* (Michoux) – (Muscadine grape or Southern Fox grape) vines of 60-100 feet long usually aerial roots berries very large and firm. Fruits mainly used for desert and culinary purposes, berries drop down at ripening.

ii) *M munsoniana* (Simpson). Little muscadine grape or everlasting grape- Slender growing vine habit berries smaller and thin skinned grape.

iii) *M. popenoei-* (Fennel)

Section 2 - *Euvitis-* Member of *Euvitis* having 38 chromosome number, bark separates from old wood in strips, diaphragm present at nodes, forked tendrils, seed pyriform, elongated clusters with berries adhere with pedicel after maturity, tendril intermittent the typical difference of American species the skin get slipped from the pulp by slight pressure.

Vitus labrusca Linn (Fox grape)

Continuous tendril, thick diaphragm, leaves pubescent beneath, long and nearly round berries purple black to reddish brown, skin thick and tough. Represented varieties of fox grape is Rhogers, Concord, Isabella.

V. lantana

It also found in the Himalayan region, berries are purple black in colour, known for crack resistance and plant resistant to disease.

V. pariviflora

Prominently found in the north western Himalayan region Kashmir to Nepal, small berries, delicately flavoured.

V. vinifera Linn (wine grape or European grape)

It is considered to have been originated primarily between Caspian and Black sea region (Vavilov, 1951). And also considered as hybrid between two American species *V. Vulpina* and *V labrusca*, which resembles *V. parriflora* and *V. lantana* found in Himalayan region, this region considered secondary centre of origin. Tendril intermittent, seeds with comparatively narrow and long beak, pulp adherent to the skin. It is native to Caucasus region and Western India. More than 90% total world production from this species *V. labrusta* and *Muscadenia* and other species of *Muscadinia* and *Euvitis* are considered to have been originated from North America, this region has largest concentration (70% of world grape diversity) hence Ericson has rightly given this region in Vine land.

V. riparia

It is found in North-Western Himalayan region, small berries, purple black in colour, cold hardy, early flowering species.

V. barbata

Prevalent in parts of Assam, Khasi hills and Bengal region of India.

V. vulpina Linn (Frost Grape)

Vigorous and tall growing vine barriers, small purple black heavy bloom.

V aestivalis Michx (summer grape)

Shoots with distinctly rusty, fruits are small in size resistant to many diseases suscepitable to phylloxora.

V. argentifolia (silver leaf grape), *V. arizonica, V. berlandieri* (Spanish grape), *V. baileyana* (possum grape) *V. californica, V. candicans, V. champini, V. cinerea, V. helleri, V. doaniana, V. gigas, V. girdiana, V. cordifolia, V. illex, V. lincecumii, V. longii, V. monticola, V. palmate* (cat grape), *V. sola, V. treleasei, V. indica, V. coignetiae, V. flexuosa, V. pentagona, V. embergeri, V. betulifolia, V. reticulate, V. armata, V. davidii, V. lanata, V. pedicellata., V. pontii* and *V. litoralis* are two new Vitis genus from Bulgaria (Kowaschew and Kovacher, 1980) *V. candicans, V. rufotomentosa,* and *V. solonis* have high degrees of resistance to nematodes.

Diversity in Indian subcontinent

The *V. parviflora V. lantana* found in the Himalayan region species resembling *V. lantana* and *V. palmata* and grows wild in the North Western Himalayan foot hills. Indigenous varieties known as Rangspay 'Shonltu White' and 'Shonltu Red' are grown even today in Himachal Pradesh.

Important cultivars of Grape

Anab-e-Shahi

It is seeded cultivar, one of the most productive cultivar grown in India and yielded over 30 tonns/acre/year. It was being extensively grown in Andhra Pradesh and Karnataka, but being replaced by Thompson Seedless, because of superior quality and seedless ness.

Cheema Sahebi

It was selected by Dr G.S. Cheema from Pandhari Sahebi at Pune, vine vigorous and heavy yielding, bunches are long and conical medium sized berries with seeded, shipping quality poor due to weak pedicel attachment.

Cordinal

It is progeny of Tokay X Ribier, developed by E. Snyder of California, USA, early, red, seeded. Vine is medium in vigour, cluster attractive, medium to large, irregular size of berries and some berries do not attain proper colour.

Black Champa

The vine are vigorous and medium in yield, purple colour bunch of excellent quality grape. The pulp is tender and sweet with mild muscat flavour. Low yield and small bunches are drawback of this cultivar.

Thompson Seedless

It is also called oval Kishmish (Mediterranean region) and Sultana (Australia). Most important cultivar for reisin production, 50% reisin produced from this cultivar alone. Tas – e- Ganesh, Chaman, Manak and Sunnaca are clone of Thompson Seedless. It respond well to cane pruning, bunch medium to large, small elongated berries are yellowish to golden after full ripe. It respond well to GA and girdling treatment.

Perlette

Typical feature is translucence of the mature berries. Perlette clearly explains its little pearl. Flesh soft and muscat flavour. High production of shot berries is major defect.

Kishmish Charni

Medium to large vine, bunches are medium to large, conical, weil to compact filled berry slightly elongated medium to large, with brick red colour. It is gaining momentum in Maharashtra as Sharad Seedless.

Delight

It is sister seedling of Perlette and early maturing cultivar with characteristic muscat flavour green small and nearly round berries with good shipping quality.

Himrod

Vine vigorous and heavy yielder, yellow green berries. The berry skin is very thick and slightly difficult to chew and berry shattering (easily separate from cluster) poor keeping and shipping quality are drawbacks.

Pusa Seedless

Selected at IARI, New Delhi from unknown origin, looks like Thompson Seedless. Superior quality, less elongated berries, good keeping quality, suitable for reisin preparation. The vine vigorous and heavy yielder. Bunch of fruit is medium with 22-24% TSS.

Dilkush

Mutant of Anab-e-Shahi promising table purpose variety.

Arka Shwetha

Black Champa X Thompson Seedless, yields 35 tones/ ha, seedless, best purple colour berry, suitable for juice preparation.

Arka Soma

Progeny of Anab-e-Shahi and Queen of Vineyard, this was released in 1994, productivity 40 t/ha, best for white desert wine preparation, bunch will filled, berry greenish yellow, round to ovoid having Muscat flavour.

Pusa Navrang

Progeny of Madeline Angevine X Rubired, early ripening basal bearing, loose bunch, resistant to anthracnose. It was released in 1996.

Pusa Urvashi

(Hur X Beauty seedless) it was released in 1997, early ripening variety, bunch loose, good for table purpose, TSS 20-22%, fairly resistant to disease.

H X Cardinal 76-1

It is an early ripening, basal bearer and productive on head as well as on bower system, bunch loose medium to big in size. T.S.S 22-23% fairly resistant to diseases.

Arka Trishna

Bangalore Blue x Convent Black. It was released in 1994, it is improvement over Bangalore Blue, vine vigorous, having high yield potential, medium bunch, very sweet (TSS 22-23^0 Brix. It is male sterile hybrid, good for vine making, good for head system of training. Resistant to anthracnose and tolerant to powdery mildew.

Some cultivars like Kishmish Charni, H-5 and Merbain Seedless have good demand in the International market.

Arkawati

(Black Champax Thompson seedless)

Arka Kanchan

Anab –e- Shahi x Queen of Vineyard.

Arka Hans

Bangalore Blue x Anab – e- Shahi.
Arka Chitra
Angoor Kalan x Anab – e- Shahi
Arka Majestic
Angoor Kalan x Black Champa

Chapter **8**

Systematic Description of Ber

Ber important member of family Rhamnaceae popularly known as Chinese date, Chinese Fig or Chinese Bore and poor man's fruit. A number of species are found in India. Ber being a very important arid zone fruit also known as King of arid fruit. It is being cultivated for fooder, fuel, fruit and timber purpose. It survive in mostly marginal land where other fruits do not do well. The systematic position of Rhamnaceae family has been discussed in chapter 7 of Grape. This chapter will cover systematic description of Ber. The order Rhamnales had already discussed in the previous chapter

Characteristic feature of Rhamnaceae Family

Family Rhamnaceae comprise 50 genera and 600 species. *Zizyphus* genus include 50 species, 18-20 belong to India.

1. Plant, shrub, tree or climber, evergreen or deciduous, spine with or without tendril.
2. Leaves simple alternate or opposite stipulated and stipules often spiny in nature. Peculier venation in which three dominant vein emerged from the base and approach to apex of leaf blade.
3. Inflorescence cymose type, flower white small bearing takes place on current and old season growth. In North Indian condition, flowering occuer in Sep-Nov and in Maharashtra during April-May.
4. Flower bisexual, rarely polygamous- deciduous, 4-5 merous, perigynous, sepals 4-5 gamosepalous, valve

concave. Stamens 5 opposite the petals free well developed intra staminal disc present. Gynoecium- carpel 3, syncarpous, ovary superior or, free, or inner, 3 locular-sometimes 2 or 1 locular with one basal ovule per locule. Fruit drupe or capsule, endosperm absent or scanty. The family comprise (*Rhamnus Genus*) include 100 species and *Zizyphus* with about 600 species (Bailey 1947).

Maheshwari and Singh (1965) recognized six economically important species in India -

India Z. *mauritiana, Z. nummularia, Z. aenopila, Z. rugosa, Z. Xylocarpus.*

Characteristics of genus *Zizyphus*

Small to vigorous tree upright or spreading growth habit, cultivated in tropical subtropical and temperate region, evergreen or deciduous, stipules are modified in curved spines, originated from cuticle region, whereas thorn has originated from vascular bundle (xylem). Well developed taproot system, three prominent basal nerve in leaves. Stipules spinous and persistent.

Important species of Zizyphus genus

Z. *mauritiana* Lamk (Indian ber). Tree spiny less than *Z.Jujuba,* leaf alternate, simple, flower borne axillary, taproot system well developed in semi-arid or arid zone. Flowering occur on old and current season shoot growth, infloresencese cymose type. Flowers hermaphrodite, actinomorphic, pentamerous or tetramerous, hypogynous intrastaminal disc present, fruit drupe round to elliptical in shape, pollination entomophilous. Time of flowering vary in different part of the country. It is totally dependent upon microclimate. In Maharashtra, where growth do not cease during winter experienced early flowering i.e. May to June and fruits are available in October, in Western Rajasthan, flowering start in July reach to peak in September. It had spreading growth habit more branching, upper side leaves, colour dark green and felted on lower side, more than 10 flowers borne in a bunch.

Z. *jujube*- (Miller) It is also known as Chinese ber or Chinese jujube, 100 percent temperate zone fruit. It is small upright tree 6-8 m height with bright green leaves glabrous on their under surface. The species is deciduous, resistant to frost.

Diversity of Zizyphous Species in India

List of species available in different part of India are as follows –

Species	Locations
Z. *apatala*, Z. *funiculosa*	Z. *incurva* North-Eastern hills
Z. *mauritiana*, Z. *nummlaria*	All over the dry tract North West India and Uttar Pradesh
Z. *oenoplia*, Z. *rugosa*	Central and Eastern India
Z. *vulgaris*	North-Western Himalaya
Z. *rupicola*	Central and Eastern India
Z *xylocarpa*	Madhya Pradesh and Pennisular Region.

Important cultivars

Early	Mid	Late
Gola, Safeda	Kaithali, Sonour 5,	Umran, Ellaichi
Narnaul, Seb	Mudia, Banarani	Pathani, ZG2.
Chanchal, Narma	Karaka, Mehroon	ZG3, Katha,
Badami, Rohtaki	Darakhi, Banarasi	Moharwali, Bhagwadi

Baranari, Delhi Gola	Kaithli, Sonour 2	Aliganj, Chameli
Banarasi Gola	Mudia.	

Ponda cultivar had biggest size fruit and Illaichi with smallest size, whereas chonchal is coloured variety.

Rescent varieties

CHE S1- It was selected from Central Horticultural Experiment Station, Godhra. CHES-1 is early bearer than Umran and Gold.

Goma Kirti

It is an early maturing ber, mature 3 weeks earlier than Umran. It is high yielding with 25.8 – 38.2% increase in yield over the control. The fruits have good keeping quality owing to earliness, it is less severely infected by fruit fly and fruit borer. It is ideal for distant marketing.

Thar Sevika

Developed by the hybridization from the cross of Seb X Katha, it is early maturing variety, fruits are juicy, sweet with a TSS content of 22-24 percent. Fruit after consumption do not cause throat sore, which is common in other cultivars. Average yield in 30-32 kg/tree.

Thar Bhujraj

A selection from local material of Bhusavar area of Bharatpur, Rajasthan. It is early maturing cultivar having an average yield potential of 30-36 kg/tree, fruits weight 27g are very juicy, sweet with a TSS of 22-23%.

Chapter **9**

Systematic description of Date Palm

Date palm is important fruit crop of arid region. In this chapter systematic pomology of Date palm will be discussed.

Classification-

Division - Phanerogams

Sub Division – Angiospermae

Class – Monocotyledones

Order – Palmales

Family – Palmae (Arecaceae)

Sub family – Phoenicaceae

Systematic position of Palmae family-

Hutchinson	**Bentham and Hooker**
	Angiospermae (Phylum)
Angiospermae (Group)	
Monocotyledons (S Phylum)	Monocotyledons (S Group)
Coroliferae (Division)	Calycinae (Division)
Palmales (order)	Palmae (Family)
Palmae (Family) (Arecaceae)	

Engler and Prantle

Angiospermae (Division)

Monocotyledoncea (Class)
Principles (Order)
Palmae (Family)

Characteristic feature of Order Palmales

1. Herbaceous stem, tall woody, sometimes climbing and armed with hooks, generally covered by persistent leaf bases.
2. Leaves often very large, entire or pinnately or flabellately divided and nerved, rachis often extended at the base in to a fibrous sheath.
3. Flower small actinomorphic, dioecious to bisexual, borne in long panicle, in large spathe like bracts, perianth double stamens usually six, superior ovary with free ovary or locules. Fruit drupe or berry seed with endosperm.
4. Plant prevalent in tropical to sub-tropical region. Under this order 250 genera and 2500 species are distributed. Three families belongs to this order Palmae, Aracaceae, Linonaceae.

Chracteristic feature of Palmae family

This family is spread over 217 genera and 2500 species (Willis, 1966), however, Eames (1961) reported the number of species as many as 4000 to 5000 in this family. In India, 25 genera and 225 species are found from this family.

1. Plant woody shrubs or tree, stem very tall erect, climbing and columnar often covered with persistent leaf base plant bear a crown of leaves at top.
2. Leaves usually form crown at the apex of stem, leaves, palmately or pinnately split, unbranched stem 50-60 m height, feather palm (*Phoenix*) or palmately (fan palm) in *Borassus* divided. The segments of leaflets folded induplicately or reduplicately in bud often sharp at apex and prickly on the margins or midrib, rachis often ex-

panded at the base into a fibrous sheath, petiole base brood.

3. Inflorescence a spadix with spath enclosing usually small flowers in large sheathing bracts (spath). Flower unisexual very rarely bisexual, actinomorphic hypogynous, sessile, leathery and fleshy perianth which may be persistent (six perianth leaves arranged in two whorls of three each).
4. Stamens 6, in two series rarely numerous. Their filaments may be connate or free anthers versatile, dehiscing by vertical slit.
5. Gynoceium, tricarperllary, apocarpous, syncarpous, superior ovary, axile placentation in trilocular ovary. In *Cocus nucifera* two carpel's abort and mature fruit contains only be easily identified by presence of three longitudinal sutures and also by the presence of three round scars on the hard endocarp of fruit. Ovary vestigial or absent in male flowers.

Fruit- type of fruit berry, drupe or nut, fruiting carpel distinct, exocarp often fibrous, sometimes covered by reflexed scales.

Important Fruits

Cocus nucifera, Metroxylon rumphii (Sagopalm Saboodona), *Areca catechu, Elaeis guinensis, Phoenix dactylifera, Phoenix sylvestris* (wild datepalm), *Borassus flabellifer* (Fan palm or Tar), *Oreodoxa regia* (Royal palm), *Calamus rotang.*

Phoenix dactylefera

1. Phoenix is only pinnate leaf genus of palm with pointed in duplicate leaflets date-palm is dioecious with a trunk of 30 m height, sucker at base with persistent leaf base and terminal crown with 4-70 m long, pinna 20-40 cm long, lower pinna converted into stout spine or petiole.

2. Inflorescence axillary much branched, enclosed in deciduous spath male inflorescence, axillary, much branched, numerous cream colour flower, 8mm long each with 6 stamens female inflorescence with 10-30 branches, pendulous fruit develop.
3. Fruit cylindrical 2.5 to 7.5 x 2.5 cm yellow to reddish brown in colour, fleshy pericarp brown in colour fleshy pericarp, seed single cylindrical long deeply grooved with hard endosperm.

Phoenix sylvestris (Wild Indian Date-palm).

It had solitary stem, it produces dry, stringent fruits, mainly uses for toddy and sugar. Sap is obtained by tapping side of crown, sap may be extracted many years without cutting of plant.

1. Tall tree (30-50 ft.), adventious root arising from the swollen base of the stem. Stem erect, columnar, covered with leaf base persistent in nature, terminal leaf crown, leaf pedicellate, pinnately compound leaf of 7-15 feet long, sheathing persistent leaf base, leaflets long and pointed lower leaflets transformed into long spine.
2. Inflorescence spadix, 2-3 feet long covered with leathery boat shaped halves of spathe.
3. flower, sessile, small, coriaceous, actinomorphic, unisexual, hypogenous, dioecious, male flower numerous and scented perianth 6 in number, stamens 6, arranged in two whorl, gynoecium, tricarpellary, apocarpous, superior, only one carperl mature ripe into fruit.

Phoenix acaulis

It is indigenous to eastern and central India, small often almost, stemless palm, commonly found in dry ground from Himalayan tract to central India.

P. humilis

Commonly found in hill forest of Kumaon region to Assam to Malabar, stem is very short, leaflet irregular spaced clusters of flower spadix long stalked.

P. rupicola

Indigenous to eastern India, Assam and Sikkim, with ornamental foliage found in lower hills of Darjeeling and Bhutan.

Important cultivars

These are more than 1000 cultivars grown all over world but only few are being extensively grown.

Soft date- Halawi, Khadrawi, Medjool, Sharman, Saidy, Hayami, these are called invert sugar date.

Soft and Semidry- Degletnoor, Barhee, Thoory, Deglet Noor, Zahidi, Dayari, retain good amount of sugar on full ripening, hence called cane sugar date.

In India date variety came from middle country and North America. In India, date fruits are harvested at Doka Stage (full grown, hard yellow or red and consumed as fresh).

Non astringent sweet variety

Halawi, Barhee

Chhuhara purpose

Kipkap, Shaker, Shahanii, Zahedi, Khadrawi, Zahidi. Zahidi is resistant to rains.

Chapter **10**

Systematic Description of Guava

Guava, the apple of tropics is fourth most important fruit of India in terms of area and production. It is commonly grown in tropical and sub tropical parts of the world. Guava had much diversity in India also. This chapter deals with systematic description of guava.

Classifications

Phylum - Phanerogams

Sub phylum - Angiospermae

Division - Lignosae

Order - Myrtales

Family- Myrtaceae.

Systematic position of Family Myrtaceae.

Hutchinson	**Bentham and Hooker**
Angiospermae (phylum)	Angiospermae (Group)
Dicotyledons (sub. phylum)	Dicotyledons (sub group)
Lignosae (Division)	Polypetalae (Division)
Mytales (Order)	Caliciflorae (series)
Myrtaceae (family)	Myrtales (order)
	Myrtaceae (Family)

Engler and Prantle
Angiospermae
Dicotyledonous (class)
Archichlamydeae (sub class)
Myrtifloreae (order)
Myrtaceae (family)

Characteristics feature of Myrtales order

1. Tree, Shrub, wood and herbaceous plants, leaves mostly opposite and often dotted.
2. Flowers usually regular, 4-5 merous and perfect type, calyx valvate, and stamens show tendency to group in bundles, sometimes dimorphous and opening by terminal pores. Ovary inferior, ovules reduced in number in higher types. Order Myrtales is spread over seven families Myrtaceae, Lecythidaceae, Rhizophoraceae, Sonneratiaceae, Punicaceae, Combretaceae and Melastomataceae.

Salient feature of Myrtaceae family

This family is spread over 80 genera and 3000 species. However, Willis and Conquest (1968) regards 100 genera and 3000 species. In India, nearly 10 genera and 130 species have been recorded.

1. Plants are mostly tree or shrub rarely climbing some species of *Eucalyptus* in the Australian Forest attain a height of 400 to 500 feet and up to 90 feet girth at base. Stem erect, woody and branched.
2. leaves generally simple, opposite rarely alternate (e.g. *Eucalyptus)* exstipulate, evergreen and entire some of the Australian species are xerophytic possessing acicular leaves.
3. Inflorescence, cymose type, sometimes solitary (e.g. *Myrtus Communis* and *Psidium guajava),* rarely racemose in *Callistemon* where they are arranged in spikes. The

cymose borne on the panicle (*Eugenia fruticosa*), axillary (*Eugenia claviflora*), *corymbose* (*Eugenia formosa*) as well as axillary 4-9 flowered umbels (*Eucalyptus teretecornis*).

4. Flower regular, actinomorphic, hermaphrodite or polygamous by abortion, complete perigynous or epigynous, two bracteales, receptacle hollow and united to the ovary, a disc is present lining the calyx tube. Calyx 4-5, free or fused, calyx tube more or less adanate to the ovary, calyx sometimes wither from base, and detach a cup shape. In case of *Eucalyptus* sepals either absent or very short in conspicuous. Corolla composed of 4-5 rarely 6 or 8 free petals rarely united inserted on the margin of disc lining of the calyx tube (leathery). Corolla sometimes thrown away bodily as a cap after opening.
5. Androecium- stamens numerous rarely few, inserted on the margins of the disc, anther small, 2 locular dorsified or versatile opening longitudinally. Gynoecium, ovary inferior, 2 to many carpillary, syncarpous, 1 to many locular, completely fused with the receptacle (ovary inferior or half inferior) axile placentation, ovules numerous anatropous or campylotropous ovule, stigma simple and capitate.

Fruit- Inferior, dehiscent or indehiscent or berry in guava. In Eugenia and Rhodomyrtus, fruit drupe like. Plants belongs to this family are *Syzygium, cumini, Psidium guajava, syzygium aromaticum, Eucalyptus sp, Callistemon lanceolatus, Myrtus Communis.*

Psidium

Nearly 150 species are grown under the genera of *Psidium. Psidium* is indigenous to tropical and sub tropical America. Leaves opposite having pinnate veins, flowers 1-3 in axillary cyme large, whitish, divided in two lobes. Calyx is not divided in two lobes, petals 4-5 spreading in free, stamens, numerous free. On broad disc. Ovary is inferior 4-5 celled with numerous ovuled, fruit is berry usually crowned with persistent calyx.

Guajava

Small tree cultivated commonly for edible fruits, plant shallow rooted shrub or small tree 3-10 m height branching close to ground and often producing suckers from the root near the trunk. Bark is smooth greenish or reddish brown, peeling of thin flakes. Young twigs are four angled and ridged, leaves are opposite glandular, petiole 3-10 mm long. Lamina elliptical to oblong glabrous above thinly pubescent beneath. Tip of leaf abtuse venation reticulate. Lateral veins 10-20 pairs, sunken above prominent below, flowers are axillary. Sometimes, solitary, or 2-3 flower in cymose type inflorescence large, white pedicellate, actinomorphic, hermaphrodite, epigynous, receptacle hollow and united to the ovary, a disc present lining to the calyx tube.

Calyx, polysepalous, leathery, caducous, persistent. Corolla, 5 petalous, showy, wither from base in form of cap after fertilization. Stamens numerous slightly connate at base inserted on the disc, ovary 4-5, locular style stigma capitate fruit berry surrounded by calyx lobes, monocarp fleshy of varying thickness, white yellow pink or red, stone cells usually present.

Cattleianum

(Strawberry guava or cattleya guava). It is native to Brazil, sometimes, it is grown for small round, purpulish red fruits of 3 cm diameter. The white flesh has sweet acid flavour, may be eaten raw or as jelly. It is small tree can be distinguished from *Guajava* by erect branchlets and smaller coriaceous, glabrous, obovate leaves. It is hardy, sub tropical species closely related to guava. This species can tolerant more low temperature than *P. gùajava.*

P. montanum

(Mountain guava) - It is found in the mountain of Jamaica, shrub, about 1.5m high, flat round branchlets.

P. friedrichsthalianum

(Chinese guava) Fruits are small and glabose shape with very high acid content. It is proved to be good root stock as it is dwarfing in nature and resistant to wilt disease and a compatible root stocks.

P. cattleianum var. Lucidium

It is sulphur yellow colour and trees are comparatively large in size (12m), fruits are mostly used for jelly preparation.

P. molla

Medium height of tree, leaves are green and oval in shape, leaf apex pointed. Red hairs are present on central veins, 6-8 pairs of primary veins found petals 5-11, stamens 196-239, stigma long with big ovary of 3-5 chamber, fruits are small in size, average fruit weight 13 g.

P. pumilum

Tree like pyramidal in shape, leaves are light colour, small size, non pubescent, 13-17 pair of primary veins, petals 7, drop immediately, stamens are 252-327 in number. If flower twice in a year, fruit weight 19 g per fruit.

P. guineense

(Guinea guava and Brazilian guava) plants are like shrub or small tree, leaves are green in colour broad, oblong-oval, acute or obtuse, 8-12 cm long with lower surface pubescent, red hairs are present on the mid veins, 8-10 pairs of primary veins present in a leaf, corolla 5-7, stamens 150-185 in number. Plant flowers round the year, small fruit (6 g weight), poor fruit quality.

P. cujavilis

It resembles to *P. guineense* in growth characters and flowering habit of plants, fruits are small to medium in size with sour taste.

P. policarpum

Growth characters resembles to *P. guajava* except fruit shape which are pyriform in shape. Fruit of big size (average weight 200-250 g per fruit).

Other species

P. chinensis

P. araca

P. littorale

P. coriaceum

P. microphyllum

Important cultivars of guava

Banarasi

It is one of the sweetest guava, lacking acidity, tree 4 to 5 m height with broad crown. Fruits round and dresden yellow medium keeping quality.

Allahabad Safeda

One of the most popular cultivar of guava from Uttar Pradesh, tree vigorous medium tall, heavy branching and dense foliage, short tendency to produce long shoots, crown broad and compact. Fruit roundish shape, medium weight, yellowish white colour fruit, good keeping quality.

Lucknow 49

It was selected from Pune by Cheema and Deshmukh in 1927 from Ganesh Khand Fruit Research Station from seedling population of Allahabad Safeda commonly known as Sardar guava, semi-dwarf tree, 2.3 to 3.4 m tall, flat common, fruit roundish ovate in shape, sweet tasty, excellent keeping quality.

Chittidar

A tall tree crown rounded spreading branches, fruit sub-globose in shape, straw yellow colour fruit, red dotted scattered on entire fruit, sweet taste and good keeping quality.

Seedless

A tall tree, long trunk, upright branch, leaves large. Fruits oblong to globose in shape straw yellow in colour, excellent keeping quality. Other seedless cultivars are Triploid Guava, Nagpur Seedless and Saharanpur Seedless.

Hisar Surkha

(Hybrid 12-34)- It was developed at CCSHAU, Hisar a progeny of Apple Colour X Banarasi Surkha, medium tree height with broad to compact crown, seeds medium in number and soft seed yield 94 kg/tree.

Hisar Safeda

(Hybrid 25-25)- A progeny of Allahabad Safeda X Seedless, it was developed from CCSHAU, Hisar. Tree medium in size, upright growth, compact grown. Fruit round weighing about 92 g, pulp creamy white with few soft seeds.

Arka Amulya

It is progeny of Seedless (Triploid) X Allahabad Safeda semi-vigrous, round, white fleshed fruit, soft seed with good keeping quality.

Arka Mridula (selection 8)

It was selected from IIHR Bangalore, from Allahabad Safeda seedling, soft seed white fleshed.

CISHG-1

It is a chance seedling selection from CISH, Lucknow, U.P. Fruit deep red, uniform size, attractive shape, only few soft seeds with long shelf life and high TSS 15^0 Brix.

CISH G3 (Lalit)

It was selected from Apple Colour seedling at CISH Lucknow, U.P., skin and flesh colour in pink.

Pant Prabhat

It was selected at G.B. Pant University of Agriculture and Technology, Pantnagar from seedling population, seeds are few and soft.

Banarasi Surkha

It is selection from Local Red fleshed type cultivar, heavy bearer and large size fruit.

Shweta

A high yielding with high total soluble solids (12.5-13.%) and good self life.

Pusa Srijan

It was identified as potential dwarfing rootstock for high density plantation. Tree size is reduced by 50 per cent, they show tolerant to guava wilt.

Chapter **11**

Systematic Description of Papaya

Papaya is a quick growing herbaceous perennial single stemmed plant. It is distributed throughout tropical and sub tropical region of world. Fruit are very delicious and plants start bearing fruit only 12 month after planting. Papaya is having very complicated fruit plants due to large number of sex form. This chapter deals with systematic description of papaya.

Classification

Phylum - Angiospermae

Sub phylum- Dicotyledons

Division- Lignosae

Order - Cucurbitales

Family- Caricaceae.

Systematic position of family Caricaceae

Hutchinson	**Bentham and Hooker**
Angiospermae (phylum)	Angiospermae (group)
Dicotyledons (sub phylum)	Dicotyledons (sub group)
Lignosae (division)	Polypetalae (division)
Cucurbitales (order)	Calyciflorae (series)
Caricacea (family)	Passifloreae (family)
	(caricaceae)

Engler and Prantle

Angiospermae

Dicotyledonea (class)

Archichlamydeas (s. class)

Apetalae.

Parietales (order)

Caricaceae (family)

Characteristics feature of Order

1. Plants generally herbaceous often climb by tendrils.
2. Stem angular with bicollateral vascular bundles, abundance of watery sap.
3. Leaves long stalked, alternate, palm-nerved, palmately lobed exstipulated.
4. Inflorescence axillary, solitary or in cymes.
5. Flower epigynous, unisexual, generally monoecious calyx lobe imbricate or valvate petals free or united rarely absent, stamens numerous to few or united ovary inferior with parietal or axile placentation.
6. Fruit soft fleshy berry, generally indehiscent.

Characteristics feature of family Caricaceae

Small family with four genera, of which 3 are indigenous to tropical and sub tropical America and one to Africa. Usually, small soft wood tree and shrub with succulent stems and trunks, which are mostly unbranched sometimes branched leaves either spirally or alternately arranged, stipulate mostly palmately lobed, rarely entirely large and mostly long petioled, forming a terminal crown. The tissues are with network of laticiferous vessels containg latex. Flowers often deciduous and sometimes polygamous.

Carica - About 48 species distributed in tropical and sub tropical America. Among all the species *carica papaya* L.

is most important and cultivated all over the world for its lucious fruits and papain. All the carica species are dioecious in nature except C. *papaya.*

Salient feature of Carica species

This family comprise four genera and 31 species viz *Carica, Facaratia, Farilla, cylicomporpha.* The edible fruit found only in C *papaya.*

C. cardamarcensis

(Mountain papaya) grows to a height of 10 m, produces multi seeded fruit through out the year which are rich juice and contain considerable amount of vitamin A and C. it is native to mountain of Colombia and Equador. It is a small sub herbaceous tree with crown of palmately lobed leaves growing to a height of 2.5 to 3.0 m and resembling cultivated *c. papaya.* The fruits are slightly longer, pendulour than *c. papaya* bearing 50-100 fruits/ tree of small elongated of oblong fruits each weighing not more than 116 g. The fruits are too acidic hence, suitable for cooking, jam and preserve preparation. This species is tolerant to frost.

C. quercifolia

It has been described by Bailey (1947) as small tree, 1.5 to 2.0m height, and in native of South America. It is hardier than *c. cardamarcensis* and can with stand a temperature as low as 2.4^{0} F, the tree bears cluster of small yellow fruits about 2.5 to 5 cm long. Although the fruits are small but reported to contain higher percentage of papain than *c papaya.*

C. monoeica

Small, three lobed leaf, glabrous thin, dark green, fruit oval in shape, 4-5 cm dia, round in cross section. It is eatable after cooking also known as Peruvian cooking papaya. The cooked leaf of this species are also used for food.

C. papaya

A short lived quick growing, soft wooded tree, 2-10 m in height, usually unbranched, small, single stemmed, evergreen quick growing plants, trunk erect hollow and hollow soft wood, leaves are large, palm like deeply lobed with long petiole. Fruits are spherical to oblong in shape, fleshy berry with central cavity, the immature fruits scratching yields white milky latex. Flowers are borne single in female and hermaphrodite or in large cluster in male in leaf axis. Plants usually dioecious but hermaphrodite may also occur, however, various scientist reported different type of sex forms. Various series occur in papaya sex forms, at one end of series lies the unisexual. Staminate flowers which has a distinctly gamopetalous. Corolla, show obscure gamopetalous that superficially appears to be polypetalous. It has large functional pistil but extremely devoid of stamens between these extreme lies numerous type mostly bisexual which differ in carpeloidy of stamens and degree of gamopetaly.

Storey (1958) classified papaya sex into 8 categories. The details are as follows –

i) staminate

ii) teratalogical staminate

iii) reduced elongata

iv) elongata

v) pentendria

vi) carpeloid pentendria

vii) carpeloid elongata

viii) pistillate.

Staminate

Typical male flowers appear in axillary panicles 25-75 cm long pendulous cluster with raceme inflorescence, the flower sessile, in complete actinomorphic, bract leafy or scaly hypogynous, funnel shape, 2.5- 3.2cm long flowers. Calyx cup shaped 1 mm long, 5 toothed, corolla in gamopetalous forming a long cylinder tube of 2/3- ¾ of its length. Stamens 10, inserted in the throat of corolla tube. The flower is unisexual and has no functional pistil although a rudimentary structure is present.

Teratological staminate

This term is used to designate certain staminate flowers which possess some degree of carpel. This type of flower found only in sex reversal type of trees.

Reduced elongata

It is staminate flowers occurs only on hermaphrodite trees. It resembles the staminate flowers morphologically but differs from it histological by having shorter, stiffer, thick walled corolla tissue.

Elongata

It is typical bisexual flower, flower appear on short pendulous cluster, petal united for 1/3 to ¾ of length forming a fairly rigid tube. As staminate flower possess 10 stamens arranged in two series. It has functional elongata pistil. Which develop more or less cylindrical fruit. Typical flower of this type contain five laterally fused carpel's.

Carpeloid elongata

This is teratological form of elongata flower. This is intermediate type flower, stamens may be carpelloid. The degree of carpelloid vary from slight to a point where the carpelloid stamens is fully developed with an ovule containing locule and astigma, the carpelloid stamens may be free or affixed with the corolla.

Pentendria

This is typical hermaphrodite flower with short corolla tube, stamens 5, by long filaments near base of ovary. Fruit developed from pentendria flowers are having 5 furrows.

Carpelloid pentendria

It is intermediate form in which the stamens become carpelloid and produce rigid or irregular shaped fruits.

Pistillate

It is a typical female flowers which do not go under sex reversion due to change in climatic condition, flowers are large sub sessile borne in the axile of the leaves, calyx 5 gamosepalous, light green, corolla five, androecium absent.

Carica papaya

Had 3 basic sex forms of viz- staminate, pistillate and andromonoecious. The pistillate is stable while staminate and andromonoecious either phenotypically stable or phenotypically ambivalent going through seasonal sex reversal. Pollen from hermaphrodite flowers are inferior to staminate flower.

Important cultivars

Washington

fruit medium to large size, round to ovate in shape, fruit weight 1 kg sweet and good flavour.

Honey Dew

This cultivar is best suitable for northern India. It is heavy bearer, fruits have less number of seeds with good flavour and taste.

Coorg Honey Dew

It is chance seedling selection from Honey Dew, hermaphrodite flower but occasionally pistillate flowers also found. It is dwarf and heavy bearer cultivars, fruits are oblong.

Pusa Delicious

It is gynodioecious cultivar, two sex form occur, hermaphrodite and pistillate are found. The fruits are medium size, deep orange colour with excellent flavour.

Pusa Majesty (Pusa 23-3)

It is also gynodioecious line medium size fruits round in shape, flesh solid in texture and yellowish in colour having good keeping quality, good transportability.

Pusa Giant (Pusa 1-45 V)

It is dioecious line and plant bears fruit at one meter height, due to its short stature can withstand to strong wind and storm, fruit attractive big size and weight ranging from 2.5 to 3.5kg/fruit.

Pusa Nanha

It is mutant of Pusa Delicious dwarf cultivar, dioecious most suitable for kichen gardening and pot cultivation and recommended for HDP. This variety is wind resistant.

Surya

It is progeny of Sunrise Solo x Pink fleshed evolved at IIHR, Bangalore, a gynodioecious line. Plants are dwarf than sunrise, solo fruits are medium size with average weight 600-800g/ per fruit, pulp is red in colour.

Solo

Fruits are pear shaped weighing 350-500 g and of excellent quality. Solo given the name by J.E. Higgins for small size fruits in Hawaii.

CO-1

It is selection from Ranchi cultivar, plant is dwarf, fruit is round or oval in shape.

CO-3

This is hybrid between CO2 X Sunrise Solo, at all vigorous plant with medium sized, sweet and good keeping quality fruits, gynodioecious cultivar.

CO-4

CO1 X Washington, plants medium tall, fruit large, good keeping quality.

CO-7

It is gynodioceious cultivar developed through multiple crosses, the parents used are Pusa Delicious, CO3, CP75 and Coorg Honey Dew. This cultivar can be grown both in plains and upto an altitude of 1000 masl.

CO-5

It was selected from Washington cultivar, dioecious in nature, best for papain production, papain can be produced in any season.

Punjab Sweet

It was developed at PAU, Punjab through Selection 86, was submitted for six generation. It is dioecious in nature, fruits are large, oblong, pointed tip, excellent flavour and taste better frost tolerant.

Chapter 12

Systematic Description of Pineapple

Pineapple known as *ananas* in Hindi is one of the commercially important fruit crops of India. The name pineapple is derived from Spanish name pina, given to the plants based on appearance of its fruits which resemble a pine cone. It is good source of carotene and ascorbic acid and is fairly rich in vitamins B and B2 viewing the importance in this chapter systematic description of pineapple has made

Classification

Sub kingdom- Spermatophyta

Class- Angiospermae

Sub-class- Monocotyledons

Order- Farinosae

Family- Bromeliaceae

Sub-family- Bromeliodieae

Genera- Ananas and Pseudananas

Systematic position of Bromeliaceae family.

Hutchninson	**Bentham and Hooker**
Angiospermae (Phylum)	Angiospermae (group)
Monocotyledons (Sub phylum)	Monocotyledons (sub group)
Calyciferae (division)	Monochylamydeae (Division)

Bromeliales (Order)
Bromeliaceae (Family)

Epigynae (series)
Bromeliaceae (Family)

Engeler and Prantle

Angiospermae
Monocotyledoneae (class)
Archichlamydeae (sub class)
Farinosae (Order)
Bromelliaceae (Family)

Characteristic feature of Bromeliaceae

A large family of American tropics, most of the members are epiphytes (they live on tree but however, pineapple is terestral.

- Mostly herbaceous plants found in tropical and subtropical region.
- Fruits syncarpous, bearing a tuft of leaves in form of crown in pineapple but no crown in *Pseudoananas*.
- Plants produces elongated stolens at base.
- Leaves spines at ascending, floral bracts coloured at maturity, plants bearing scales.
- Plants like small shrubs, basal leaves long slender.
- Inflorcescence panicle, raceme, often terminal spike with highly coloured bracts, flower regular or bisexual.
- Fruit berry or capsule, syncarpous or sorosis. This family comprise 900 species.

Characteristics feature of *Ananas* genus

i) Plants are like small shrub epiphyte, basal leaves spiny, slender, triangle like sheathing at base, tuff and spiny herbaceous perennial, self sterile monocotyledonous plant. Leaves are long and narrow and are arranged in a right or left handed spiral on a short stem.

ii) Inflorescence panicle, receme often terminal spike with highly coloured bract. The plants bears a single fruit terminally on a peduncle, protruding out from the centre of rosette.

iii) Flower regular or bisexual, perianth 6 in stamens 6 mostly attached to base adanate to whole length, ovary 3 celled.

iv) Fruit berry or capsule, fruit syncarpous multiple fruits formed by the fusion of fruit lets, produced by each flower. The multiple fruit mature 5-6 months after flowering.

v) Plants bears a total of 100-200 reddish purple flowers, arranged spirally on the axis, each subtended by a floral bract. Each flower had two perianth whorls, an outer of 3 free, short calyx and inner 3 larger petals and a narrow style with three lobed stigma, and six stamens. The inferior ovary has 3 united carpels with 1015 ovules in each of the 3 loculi. Normally, flowers are self sterile and fruits develop parthenocarpically but cross pollination between varieties results in normal fertilization and production of seeds.

Important Cultivars

1. **Cayenne group-** The varieties of Cayenne group are used for dual purpose. It is very vigorous group, leaves are without spines, plants are stocky and robust with tapering fleshy of leaves. The fruits are cylindrical in shape and weight between 2 and 3 kgs, the fruitlets (eys) are typically broad and flat. Cultivars are Hilo, Kew, giant Kew, Charlotte Rothschild. These cultivars are most widely grown for commercial production and caning purpose.

2. **Spanish Group-** Mostly cultivated as dual purpose, it is important in tropical America, it is hardiest among all cultivars Red Spanish, Singapore Spanish, Masmerah.

3. **Queen Group-** Queen group are grown exclusively for fresh fruit markets as they are not suitable for canning, owing to deep eyes. Queen or Common Queen, Mauritius, Ripley Queen, Alexandra, Mac Gregor and Queen.

Queen Species

Earlier *Ananas* was considered as a monotypic genus including many cultivars with a single species, Smith (1979) established two genera, *Anana* and *Pseudoananas* (Crown fruit). The *Ananas* comprise 8 genus.

1. *Ananas cosmosus*
2. *A. monstrosus*- No crown on the fruit (Crownless).
3. *A. bracteatus* – It had well developed bright red flower bracts, fruits are relatively large and edible and seeded.
4. *A. fritzmuelleri*- Leaf spine recurved towards base bract. The petals bear special appendices found only in the neighboring genus *pseudomonas.* Fruits are fleshy and seeded.
5. *A. ananassoides*- It is with small fruit erect leaves and a long fairly thin spike. Fruit become dry at maturity with little flesh.
6. *A. nanus*- It is dwarf and phenotypically resembled to *A. ananassoides.*
7. *A. paraguazensis*- It also resembled to *A. ananassoides,* but the different features are its curved leaves.
8. *A. lucidus*- It also similar to *A. ananassoides* has smooth (spineless) leaves from which good quality fibre can be obtained.

Chapter 13

Systematic Description of Fig and JackFruit

Classification

Phylum- Angiospermae

Sub phylum- Dicotyledonous

Division- Lignosae

Order- Urticales

Family- Moraceae.

Characteristics feature of Urticales order

1. Mostly tree, shrub or herbs sometimes epiphytic.
2. Leaves, mostly alternate and generally stipulated.
3. Flower bisexual or unisexual, calyx small without petals, stamens few, erect or inflexed in bud. Ovary superior, 1-2 locular, ovule solitary, erect or pendulous seeds with or without endosperm. This order comprises six families i.e Ulmaceae, Urticaceae, Cannabaceae, Barbeyaceae, Moraceae, Eucommiaceae. The crop fig and jackfruit belongs to family Moracea, hence its systematic position need to be given.

Systematic position of Moraceae as per taxonomist.

Hutchinson	**Engler and Prantle**
Angiospermae (phylum)	Angiospermae
Dicotyledons (sub phylum)	Dicotyledonea (division)
Lignosae (Division)	Archichlamydeae (Sub division)

Uritcales (order)	Urticales (order)
Moraceae (family)	Moraceae (family)

Benthan & Hooker

Angiospermae (group)
Dicotyledones (Sub group)
Monochlamydeae (division)
Unisexuals (order)
Moraceae (family)

Salient feature of Moraceae family

1. Moracea is small family comprise 70 genera and 1000 species. Plants are distributed in tropical region but few may occur in temperate and sub tropical climatic conditions.
2. Plants are tree shrub rarely herbs, some of them are epiphyte (*ficus* sp) or climbing in habit (e.g *ficus benjamina).* Mostly well developed taproot system but in *ficus benghalensix* and *F. elastica* aerial roots are found which reach the ground and act as support or as well as absorptive organs.
3. Stem mostly erect, woody and branched, latex cells are present in most of the plants contained mostly in secondary cortex or phloem which exude white milk substance. Leaves alternate rarely opposite, stipulate, usually simple, entire serrate or lobed petiolate leathery. Stipules may be free or in lateral and prominent, and petiole interpetiolar *(F. carica)* or two opposite stipules may fused to form cap over the developing buds for defence purpose.
4. Inflorescence mostly cymose type, which often condensed to form a compact head; usually catkins in which male female flower borne on different shoots known as hypanthodium where, the receptacle forms a flask-shaped structure and the unisexual flower borne

on its inner surface. Flowers are very small numerous in number, monoecious, tetramenous, actinomprhic with persistent perianths, generally become succulent and hypogynous. In male flowers, perianth four lobed arranged in two whorl, free but connate below stamens corresponding to the number of perianth lobes, arranged opposite to the perianth lobes, anther two celled versatile dehiscing longitudinally.

5. Female flower bicarpellary, syncarpous, superior to inferior ovary position. Ovule only one, pendulous rarely basal and orthrotropous stigma one or bifid.
6. Fruit drupe with fleshy perianth, mostly aggregated composite known as syconus. However, in case of *artocarpus* fruit, the perianth and the axis become fleshy and fused together to form single solid fruit. In case of *Morus* individual fruit can be distinguished and are enclosed in fleshy perianth, collectively fruits are known as sorosis.

Plants belong to family Moraceae

Ficus carica

F. religiosa

F. benghalensis

F. glomerata

F. alba

Antocarpus lakboocha

A. heterophyllus

F. elastica

F. hispida (fibre yielding plants)

Salient feature of important species of *Morus genera*

1. ***Morus alba*** (White mulberry) - It is native to China and grown in many parts of tropics. The fruits may be fresh eaten or may be eaten after cooking. This species mostly grown for its leaf to rear the silk worm. In China, its

barks are used for making paper. Wood is used for sport goods manufacture such as rachet, hockey sticks etc. Tree small with thin oval and serrated leaf often deeply lobed, monoecious or dioecious; the female spike produce a syncarpous of 2.5-5 cm long fruit comprising druplets enclosed in many perianth. They may be white, purple, red or black in colour.

M. nigra - (Black mulberry)- This species abundantly found on higher elevation.

2. ***Artcarpous* genera** -In the genus of small to large evergreen trees distributed from Sri Lanka and India to South China and through Malaysia to Solomon island. This genus contain 50 species, however, 9 species have been recorded in India. The species *A. heterophyllus* lam in grown for their edible fruits and *A. chaplasha* Roxb. are important timber tree.

Salient feature of Artocarpus

1. All plant parts having thick latex.
2. leaves are simple sometimes are pinnate.
3. large stipules covering bud.
4. Flowers are minute and numerous in number and are set on fleshy rachis.
5. Male inflorescence are axillary borne near the end of the twig.
6. Flowers are having small calyx and one stamens.
7. Female inflorescence borne singly in leaf axils or on trunk and branches, female inflorescence often large size and prickly flowers are single ovary and long style.
8. Compound fruits technically known as sorosis emerged from main trunk such character is known as cauliflory.

A. integra* and *A. integrifolia

A heterophyllus: - (2n=56) are synonyms commonly

known as Jackfruit is one of the most popular fruits of South India. The tree is indigenous to the evergreen forests of the Western Ghats at altitudes of 450-1200 m amsl but seen growing throughout other hotter part of India too. Jack fruit evergreen, monoecious tree, reaches up to 20 m height, well developed tap root system due to which it could not bear transplanting shock. Plant produce white resin latex in all plant parts. Twigs are glabrous, stipules oval triangular 2-7 cm long. Leaves are spirally arranged usually glabrous young leaf have 2-3 pairs lobes. Male inflorescence are borne axillary on leafy twig or from trunk, branches but above male inflorescence. Female inflorescence are drooping oblong 5-10 cm long 2-3 cm thick, numerous flowers are dense minute with too lobed calyx and single stamens. Female inflorescence borne on short twigs or on main trunk and branches. Peduncle stout with green fleshy ring at apex. They are larger than male flower. Small calyx tubular ovary, oblong and compact style terminate and stigma inclavett. Fruit zygotic, syncarp, the biggest of all cultivated fruits, 30-90 cm long and 25-50 cm diameter. Fruit barell or pear shaped glabrous with sharp hexagonal flesh, spike, rind yellow, flesh yellow and waxy seeds with thick gelatinious yellow covering.

*A. **Chaplasha***- Distributed in the moist deciduous and evergreen forests of the sub-Himalayan tracts from Nepal eastward to West Bengal, Assam and Tripura. It is an important constituent of evergreen and deciduous forest of Andaman and Nicobar Islands.

*A. **cummunis***- It is commonly called as bread fruit is found mostly in Western Coast and Western Ghats. There are two cultivars, one is seeded type and other seedless, seeded type had little economic value.

*A. **hirustum***- It is commonly found in the evergreen forests of Western Ghats from Konkan southward is fairly common in North Kanara and Kodagu in Karnatka to Kerala where it is very important tree. It require heavy rainfall 174 cm anuualy and thrive well on laterite soil at the foot of the Ghats. The tree can withstand at shade but thrive best with a fair amount of light.

A. Lakoocha- (Monkey Jack)- It is in wild state found in the moist or deciduous forests along the bank of streams and along the site of moist ravines. It is found distributed in evergreen, semi- evergreen and moist deciduous forests up to an altitude of 1800 m in eastern and western India. It is also found growing in Andaman island.

Fig (Ficus carica)- Fig is a small shrub to large tree. Inflorsence in hypanthodium (synconium) which is unique to this genus *ficus* containing hollow vase shape peduncle inside which are implanted the flower. It had narrow mouth hole known as ostiole which is closed with interlocking scales. Fruit is usually false type developed from syconium. Fig is a small tree, deciduous in nature, leaf large, broadly ovate, more or less deeply lobed (3-5 lobes). Flowers are numerous, tiny, unisexual, female flower single carpel, containing one ovule usually a bifig stigma and long and short styled fruit is botanically drupe usually. According to sex of flower in syconium it is of two type i) Caprifig ii) True Fig.

Caprifig- In caprifig the syconia contain short styled pistillate flowers distributed over most of the inner wall. Staminate flower mased around interior of the ostiole. Caprifig is primitive fig which has functional staminate flowers, bears non edible fruits as the flowers are pollinated by a wasp *Blastophaga psenes* harbour in the fruit.

True fig- The true fig contain only long styled pistillate flower. It is edible type fig may be classified in following groups.

i) Common fig ii) Smyrna fig iii) Sanperdro fig.

Common fig (Adriatic fig)- Generally produce one crop in a season but some cultivar may produce two batches of flower; for fruit development, pollination is not necessary.

Smyrna fig- It bears two batches of flowers in a year i.e. March-April and September-October. The second flush bears fruit only, since the pollination is successful in that season only. Pollination is imperative for fruit production, fruits are seeded. Pollination took place by caprifig technically known as Caprification.

Sanpedrofig- It also produces two batches of flower in a year. The first crop develop parthenocarpically known as Breba, is seedless fruit. The second crop require pollination for fruit development.

The Smyrna fig is important in Europe and United States the important cultivars are Kandota, Bianco Grasso, Nutty Flavour. In India, common (Adriatic) fig is cultivated which is supposed to the hybrid between *F. carica* and indigenous species, the cultivated varities in India are Pune, Billary, Gangam Marseilles etc. Recently, Indian Institute of Horticultural Research (Bangalore) introduced few exotic cultivars. Among these cultivars, Deanna, Conadria and Excel are performed better.

Chapter **14**

Systematic description of Litchi (Queen of the Fruits)

Classification

Phylum – Angiospermae

Sub-phylum- Dicotyledones

Division:- Lignasae

Order:- Sapindales.

Salient features of Sapindales order

i) Order sapindales comprise trees or shrubs. Leaves mostly compound, usually pinnate, rarely digitate, not gland- dotted, stipules rarely occurs.

ii) Flowers hypogynous or slightly perigynous, often polygamous or unisexual sepals imbricate, petals, present generally disc. Ovary superior, with rarely numerous ovules in each locules, axile placentation. Seeds mostly non-endospermic. This order consist of 11 families. Melianthaceae Sapindaceae, Sabiaceae, Podoaceae, Anacardiaceae, Aceraceae, Hippocastanaceae, Staphyleaceae, Akanianceae, Julianicaeae and Didiereaceae.

Systematic position of Sapindacea

Hutchinson	**Bentham amd Hooker's**
Angiospermae (phylum)	Angiosperms (groups)
Dicotyledons (Sub Phylum)	Dicotyledons (Sub group)

Lignosae (Division)	Polypetalae (division)
Sapindales (order)	Thalamiflorae (series)
Sapindaceae (family)	Sapindales (order)
Napheleae (Sub-family)	Sapindaceae

Engler & Prantle

Phanerogams

Dicotyledoneae (class)

Archichlamydeae (Sub class)

Sapindales (order)

Sapindaceae (family)

The sapindaceae or soapberry family consist about 150 genera and more than 2000 species mostly tropical and subtropical fruits. Important member to which belongs to this family are:

Euphoria longana Lam.

Nephelium Lappaceum L

Niphelium mutabilis

Genus Litchi has two species *Litchi Chinensis* and *L. philippinesis and L. Javensis.*

Salient feature of Litchi

1. Trees grows to a height of 6-9m with spreading branches and a dense light green shining foliage. The leaf is compound mostly paripinnate with three pairs of leaf lets. Leaves arranged alternatively, exstipulate, petiolated leaf. The trees are long lived, round topped, handsome, evergreen tree leaflets 2-9 opposite or nearly in some case a few alternate. Lanceolate to oblong-lancealate, entirely or slightly wavy, acute or acuminate, dark green and quite glabrous average size 13.50 cm long and 4.15 cm wide entire or slightly wavy acute or acuminate dark green and quite glabrous.

2. Flower borne on the axis of the 3rd order rarely on 4th and occasionally on the main axis in form of inflorescence. Inflorescence consist several multiple branched essence consist several multiple branched panicles. It has complete racemose type of inflorescence. Inflorescence develop from terminal and axillary buds. Flowers are small, apeatalous, male, pseudo hermaphrodite (Functional male) and hermaphrodite. The mature litchi fruit single seed nut usually develops in bunch. The fruit pericarp is papillate like strawberry and turns pinkish red when fruit ripe. The aril is an edible portion of fruit, which is an outgrowth of the outer cell layers of the seed coat (outer integument) which separate, easily lies under the pericarp and completely surrounds the seeds. The seeds are dark brown colour.

Important Litchi Cultivars

Early Seedless

An earliest maturing cultivar mainly grown in Uttar Pradesh and Punjab, tree of medium vigour, attain an average height of 5m and spread of 6.2m regular bearer, medium to low yielding (50-60 kg/ tree). Fruits are small to medium size, heart to oval shape, rarely globose, surface rough, seeds are very small.

Muzaffarpur

It is one of the important cultivar, bears profusely; the fruits are deep orange to pink in colour. Average weight of fruit is 20g, pulp sweet and tough, moderately juicy with good flovour.

Rose Scented

One of the most popular litchi varieties grown in India. Besides, high fruit quality, it is famous for distinct rose aroma, hence called Rose Scented. It is mid season variety. Average yield 80-90 kg per tree, fruit are mostly oval or oblong, conical in shape, deep rose pink in colour, average weight 20-24 g, seed is small.

Shahi

This is commercial cultivar of Muzaffarpur area of Bihar. Fruits are oval and oblong, conical in shape which matures in the third week of May. At maturity the tubercles are crimson- red colour with uranium- green background. Fruit are generally large size. It is heavy and regular bearing cultivars suitable for canning purpose.

Calcutta

It is best variety grown throughout north part of India. It is also partly too resistant, and can be grown in hotter area successfully provided there are protection from hot and strong wind and irrigation facility. It is late maturing cultivar, profuse regular bearing, 80-100 kg per tree yield, fruits are large in size.

Late Seedless

This is a deceptive name as the fruits are not completely seedless. The seed is rather shriveled and small in size. It is late season variety. The average yields varies from 80 to100 kg per tree. Fruits are medium to large in size.

Dehra Dun

Principle variety of Uttar Pradesh and Punjab. In Bihar, it is cultivated under the name of the Dehra-Rose. It is also a late season variety and fruit starts ripening in the third week of June. Medium to high yielding tree of 80-90 kg/tree.

Gulabi

It is late season variety of north India. It bears profusely and regularly with 90-100 kg fruit per tree, fruit oval to oblong and heart shaped.

Swarn Roopa

This cultivars was evolved from Central Horticultural Experiment Station, Ranchi, it is most promising variety of Litchi, resistant to cracking high yielding and late in maturity.

Sabour Madhu (H-105)- A progeny of Purbix Bedana.

Sabour Priya (H-73)- Purbi X Bedana both hybrids were released from Bihar Agricultural College, Sabour for commercial cultivation.

Chapter 15

Systematic Description of Custard Apple

Classification

Phylum- Angiospermae

Sub-phylum- Dicotyledons

Division - Lignosae

Order - Annonales

Salient feature of Annonales Order

1. Mostly woody tree, leaves alternate, simple, and exstipulate, mostly occur in tropical and sub tropical areas.
2. Flowers hypogynous to perigynous, bi-sexual, petaliferous with occasional gamopetaly stamens free, carpel apocarpous to rarely syncarpous with parietal placenta. Endosperm markedly ruminate with minute embryo.

This order include two families Annonaceae and Eupomatiaceae.

Systematic position of annonaceae family according to taxonomist.

Hutchinson	**Engler & Prantle**
Dicotyledonous (Sub Phylum)	Dicotyledonae (class)
Lignosae (Division)	Archichlamydeae (Sub-Class)
Annonales (order)	Ranales (order)
Annonaceae (Family)	Annonaceae (family)

Bentham & Hooker

Dictoyledons (Sub Class)

Polypetalae (Division)

Thalamiflorae (series)

Ranales (order)

Annonaceae (family)

Salient feature of Annonaceae family

1. Mostly tree or shrub with alternate simple and exstipulated leaves. Glabrous entire, dotted gland leaf, deciduous or persistent, unicostate, reticulate venation.
2. Inflorescences solitary, axillary or cauliflorae type flower produced.
3. Flower large, pedicellate, bisexual, sometimes unisexual, trimerous, rarely dimerous, floral parts spirally arranged, hypogynous, sometimes perigynous. Flowers are yellowish and hermaphrodite, sepals 3, petals 6. Sometimes 3, perianth 3 or more aestivation in outer whorl valvate and in inner whorl imbricate. Stamens numerous, rarely few, spirally arranged over a raised receptacle, filament short, anthers 4 called. Multicarpellary, apocarpous sometimes syncarpous, spirally arranged in the convex receptacle, superior ovule, one to many per carpels, placenta, marginal or basal.
4. Fruit is an etaerio of berries united to receptacle forming a single fruit. Seed large embryo small surrounded by ruminate endosperm.
5. Flowers are pollinated by beetle; fruit setting is often very poor and usually increase by hand pollination dichogamy (Protogeny) condition found. The ripe fruits are soft perishable and ferment quickly. This family is spread over about 80 genera and 850 species (Lawrence, 1964). Takhtajan (1966) included 120 genera and 2100 species. In India, 129 species are found.

The genus *Annona* contains some 120 species and 40 genera. Species originating from warm countries but some important species has got extreme important being called over the name of great god and goddess. Important species are as follows.

A. squamosa- Sweet sop, sharifa and Sitaphal

A. cherimola- Lakshmanphal, it is found in cooler places in India.

A. atemoya- Progeny of *A. Squamosa x A. cherimola.* It is a adopted to cooler climate and alkali soil.

A. reticulata- Ramphal or Bullock's heart as root stock.

A. glabra- Pond apple- used as root stock

A. muricata- Sour sop or Hanumanphal being used as root stock. It is found in mountain region of India.

A. mantna Mountain soursap- Being used in breeding programme for quality enhancement.

A. purpurea (Soncoya)- Being used as resistant source for fruit cracking.

A. scleroderma (Eoshto)- Used in breeding programme for thick hard shell.

A. diversifolia

cherimata:- A progency of *A. squamosa* X *A. cherimola.*

Characteristic feature of important species

A. cherimola- (Mill) Cherimoya considered to be the most delicious of the annonaceous fruits has an excellent quality pulp with a sub acidic and lucious buttery consistency and melt on the tongue. It is small erect tree, somewhat deciduous tree rarely grow over 7.5 pH. Generally found in Peru. Fruit is heart shaped, conical, oval or irregular in form and weight 150 to 2000g. Fruit skin thin delicate, light green and smooth are covered with small conical lumps. Flesh is slightly white acidic and has a delicate flavour of pineapple and banana. Fruit comprise numerous brown colour seed. Cherimoya is the only species adapted to tropical, sub tropical highland conditions. Cherimoya is reported to be especially sensitive to dry wind.

A. muricata L. (A *bonphandiana* Kunth, *A. cearensis* (Barb) Rodr., A. *macrocana* (Werckle), *A. muricata* var. *borinquensis* , Morales, *Guahnabonus muricaius* Gomez) - Sour sop small evergreen, cylinder tree rarely over 6m height. Widely cultivated from cnetal America to Coastal valley of Pery. Furits are often distorted and kidney shape due to some ovule not fertilized, white flesh and acidic nature, aromatic, contain many black seeds.

A. reticulata L (A. *excelsa* Kunth, *A. laevis* Kunth, A. *longifolia* Moc and Sesse, *A . riparia* Kunth)- Bullock's heart.

A *squamosa* (*A. asiatica)* Custard apple, sugar apple, sweet sop, sitaphal- A small tree of height 5m. It is native to West Indies and South America and grown on tropics also on lower altitude. Fruit around heart shaped ovoid conical, 5-7.5 cm diameter and yellowish green in colour, furit surface is covered with rounded fleshy tubercles, which represent the loosely cohering caprels and separated readily when ripe; granular pulp surrounds the small brown glossy seeds. Custard apple cultivars are Mammoth Seedless, Balanagar Barbados, British Guinea, Brandy, Islander, Red Sitaphal, Washington, Local Sitaphal.

Cheri mola cultivars

Finger Printed Cherimoya

Smooth Cherimoya,

Tuberculate

Mammillate Cherimoya

Atemoya Cultivars

African Pride

Pink Mammoth

Neilson

Island Gem

African Pride

Bradley

Keller

Page

APK-1

It is clonal selection from a high yielding type (14.9 kg/ Tree), available at the State Horticultural Form, Courtallaim, from Regional Research Station, Aruppukottai, T.N. in 2003.

Arka Sahan

It is progeny of Island gem (*A. atemoya* Hort.) X Mammoth (*A. squamosa*). Fruits are ready to harvest in September-October and mature fruits (210 g) take about 6-7 days to ripe. The skin has a waxy bloom, light green in colour, moderately thick (0.5 cm) with large flat segments. Average yield 12 tonnes of fruit/hectare. Suitable for drought prone area. Fruit exhibits long shelf life.

Chapter **16**

Systematic Description of Pome and Stone fruits

Classification

Phylum- Angiospermae

Sub phylum- Dicotyledons

Division- Lignosae

Order- Rosales

Salient feature of Rosales order

1. Mostly tree, shrubs or herbs.
2. leaves alternate, rarely opposite, simple or compound, stipules present rarely absent.
3. bisexual flower, actinomorphic, petals free. Stamens perigynous to epigynous, mostly free. Carpels free or variebly united and ovary often inferior. Seed devoid of endosperm.

The order Rosales include families i.e. Rosaceae, Dictapetalaceae and Calycanthaceae.

Systematic Position of Rosaceae family as per taxonomist.

Hutchinson	Engler & Prantle
Angiospermae (Phylum)	Angiospermae
Dicotyledons (Sub Phylum)	Dicotyledoneae (Class)
Lignosae (Division)	Archichlamydeae (Sub class)

Rosales (Order)
Rosaceae (Family)

Bentham and Hooker
Dicotyledones (Sub group)
Polypetalae (Division)
Calciflorae (series)
Rosales (Order)

Rosales (order)
Rosaceae (Family)
Angiospermae (Group)

Characteristics feature of Rosaceae

1. Plants are annual, perennial, herb, shrubs or tree rarely climber (*Frageria* sp.)
2. Stem herbaceous or woody, underground modified stem such as sucker or runner are useful in plant multiplication
3. leaves, stipulated, sometimes adnate to the petiole eg *Rosa* and *Rubus* Sp; leaves alternate or very rarely opposite simple pinnately compound, sometimes both simple and compound leaf may found in one genus.
4. Inflorescence are of many types, flowers may borne solitary (single), axillary or few in axillary cyme (*frageria)* terminal cyme, terminal spike like raceme, terminal corymb, axillary or terminal panicle.
5. flower bearing axis (receptacle) in flat cup shaped, often convex in the middle. Perigynous, sometimes epigynous wing to fusion of the carpels with receptacles. Flowers large showy and scented. Epicalyx represents the stipules of the sepals. Sepals 5 or 4, gamosepalous or baselly connate, few sepals turning into foliaceous green imbricate or valvate. Petals 5 or multiple of 5, polypetalous, petals rosaceous larger, coloured and scented, imbrical petals many in cultivated species. Since the stamens get transformed into petals, stamens bent inward, stamens are two three or four times as many as the number of petals or indefinite, perigynous

arranged one or many whorl. Rarely connate, anther small and didymous. Stamens are arranged in monoadelphous, polyadelphous, anther split longitudinally. Between stamens and carpels a ring like cushion shaped nector secreting disc is present. The thalamous may be fleshy, conical or domeshaped (hypogynous in *Pyrus* hollow cup shape in *Rosa* sp or flask shaped completely enclosing the carpels (*Pyrus* sp carpels one two or three, 2-5 fused, 5 free, polycarpellary, free usually superior and apocarpous with basal placentation. (in *Pyrus* there are single carpel, *Pyrus* had 3-5 carpels, syncarpous ovary, however, in *Potentilla fruticosa,* there are indefinite fused carpels. Fruit are drupe, an etario of drupe or an achene, pome or aggregate of small drupes in *Rubas,* or berry in Loquat.

Family Rosaceae contain 115 genera and 3200 species (Lawrence, 1964), however Willis (1966), described 100 genera and 2000 species and Gonguli (1968) mentioned, 3000 species.

Systematic description of Apple

Apple is the member of Family Rosaceae; sub family Pomoideae.

1. Small to large tree or shrub type with well developed taproot system and suckering habit may found., stem, woody erect and branched.
2. Leaf petiolated, simple, stipulated, stipules are caduceus in nature.
3. Floral inflorescence are in umbellate cyme, flower actinomorphic, hermaphrodite, regular, epigynous, white in colour. Calyx 5, gamosepalous reflexed, bell-shaped, green in colour, persistent, becoming enlarge and fleshy in fruit. Corolla also 5 in number, shortly clawed, alternating with the sepals white or light pink in colour. Stamens indefinite or 20 when more in number

are arranged in three whorls, outermost whorl of 5 pairs of antisepalous stamens, all free, anthers slightly curved. Carpel 3-5 in number, syncarpous hypanthium (cup shaped expansion of floral axis, ovary adanate throughout its inner part two ovule in each carpel, style 4-5, stigma terminal.

Fruit more or less fleshy, pome, the fleshy being derived from the enlarged hypanthium, which enclose the bony, leathery or papery carpel. Pome is a pseudocarp consisting of large, fleshy torus having 4-5 parchment like cells at the centre of fruit, each cell contain one or two seeds; the seeds are non-endospermic. Fruits are subglobose of varying size, shape and colour with slight to prominent depression at either end.

The apple which are grown mostly belongs to the species *Malus,* Linnaeus placed in genera of pear and name become *Pyrus malus* L. recently Britton has separated it from pear genus on the ground that flesh in free from girt cells and given botanical name *Malus / malus* (Britton) but Borkh given *Malus domestica.*

The genus *Malus,* a small deciduous tree of the north temperate zone distributed in both hemisphere three or four species including cultivated have been recorded in India. However, the important species belongs to this genus are included under these genera.

Malus bacccata (Linn). Borkh *Pyrus beccata, P. baccata* var *siberica* (Siberian Crab apple). A small round headed tree, short trunk, simple or branched spines when old, leaves tomentose or glabrous serrulate flower white, fruit subglobose 1-3 cm in dia, fruits are red, scarlet yellowish green, with few white spots borne on long slender pedicels. Four or five species have been recognized including the Indian form. *M. bocata* var *Himalayca* (Maxim), Schneid, Himalayan crab which is found in the temperate Himalaya from Kashmir and Kumaon to Bhutan, and Khari and Jaintia hills in Assam (Wealth of India).

M. baccata **var. Himalaica (Maximum) Schneid-** Found in wild form at 3000m amsl in Himachal Pradesh and 1303m amsl in Meghalaya, grows wildly in Uttranchal (Srivastava, *et al.* 1977) where it is used as dwarfing rootstock. Red coloured fruits, plants are partly resistant to collar rot, root rot and wooly aphid.

M. baccata (Linn.) Borkh (Khrot)

Locally known as Banphal in H.P., grows at 2000 m amsl tree low, spreading, produce, small yellow fruits with red strips, as dwarf as M-9, good graft compatible.

M. baccata (Linn.) (Srinagar)

Found wild at 1390 m amsl, Srinagar. Tree semi-dwarfing in vigour, small yellow coloured fruits.

M. sikkimensis (Hook. F.) Kochneex Schneider

It is similar to *M. baccata,* but fruits are somewhat larger and moderately serrate leaves and speckled fruits. This species is found in the Sikkim hills and in Bhutan (2100-3000 m), this produce apomictic seedlings. Other spicies which produces apomictic seedlings are *M. toringoides* and *M. hupehensis.*

M. coronaria L. (American crab apple)- This a fragrant crab. The flowers are large, showy or slender, pedical, white or rose coloured and delightfully fragrant. Leaves avate to triangular ovate and often 3 labed. Fruit with diameter of 1-1 ½ inch, persistent calyx, fruit ripens late, sour and bitter.

M. angustifolia Ait

(Narrow leaved crab apple)- It is native of the southern states is much like *M. coronaria* except that its leaves are not lobed but are lanceolate ablong and acute at the base, flowers are pink in colour, very fragrant, calyx persistent, fruit about one inch diameter, pale green or yellowish colour ripens in winter.

M. floribunda (flowering crab apple)

It is native of japan, the trees are small and thorny. Flowers are highly ornamental, rose red colour. Fruits are small and red in colour.

M. ioensis

Trees small, flowers are large, fruits are green with light coloured spots.

M. soulardii

It is natural hybrid of *M. sylvestris* and *M. ioensis*. The trees are small, fruits are large with good aroma.

M. baccata (Linn.) Borkh (Shillong)

Found wild growing in Shillong (Meghalaya) at 1300 m amsl, locally called 'Soh Sheur' in Himachal Pradesh. Plants are small low branching with small scarlet red fruits. Used as dwarfing root stock, easily multiplied by mound layering, high degree of resistant to powdery mildew, woolly aphid and field tolerant to apple scab.

M. sylvestris

The trees are large, it is considered to be the native of western Asia and South east Europe.

M. domestica

It is mostly cultivated species, a low round-crowned tree, usually up to 15m height with tomentose or heavily pubscent young growth leaves mostly clustered on short shoots or spurs ovate or elliptic to broad elliptic, 4.5 to 10 cm long soft texture, blundetly serrated margins fruits small to big in size.

An historical analysis of apple nomenclature leads to the conclusion that the legitimate pithet for cultivated apple is *M x domestica* Borkh. (Korban and Skirvin, 1984).

M. baccata (Linn.) Borkh (Giabung)

This species was collected from Giabung (H.P.) at an altitude of 2060 m amsl. Fruits are small scarlet red coloured.

M. baccata (Linn.) Borkh (Rohru)

This was locally collected from Rohru (H.P.). Trees are small and bushy, on the basis of stomatal density, it revealed that root stocks may be more dwarf than M-9, moderately resistant to powdery mildew.

New Malus Species

M. dirangensis

It is new crab apple from Arunachal Pradesh. It had used as root stock and 85 percent success was obtained when budded onto 3 month old seedlings of *M. dirangensis*; This species can also be multiplied by stem cutting (Joshi and Singh, 1980).

M. bulgarica

It is closely related to *M. sieverii, M. rhodopaea,* similar to *M. sylvestris, M. aprilovii* (Dimitirov *et al*; 1980].

M. *boccata* Linn. Sub species *columnaris*

It is small stature with no or little branching, Column is the *Malus* cultivar which grows so narrowly, fruits are yellow with a large red cheeks, I bears fruit regularly.

M. baccata* sub species *Gracilis

Plants are shrubby in nature, slow growing thin branched, dense, leaves small narrow, long acuminate, flower small, white, buds, pink fruits are of small nearly pea sized and pear shaped.

***M. brevipis* (Rehd)**

Trees are of compact with stiffy branched, twigs stiff

usually only a shrub, leaves like those of *M. floribunda* 5-7 cm long, fairly and densely serrated. Flowers numerous, nearly pure white, flower stalk glabrous, fruit 2 cm thick, bright red somewhat ribbeedon a stiffy erect, reddish stalk.

M. floribunda (Van Houte)

Plants are shrub or tree in nature 4-10 m height crown dense, twigs usually nodding to wide spreading, young shoot slender, reddish on many sides, pubescent leaves folded in bud stage, ovate 4-8 cm long , acuminate, sharp seriata, fruit yellow pea sized.

M. formosana

It is deciduous tree 12m height, young shoots often thorny, leaves irregular serrate, base round or curate with 9-11 veins pairs, pubescent when young, fruits broadly oval 4-5cm thick with persistent calyx.

Origin of *M. domestica*. - Recent studies on the origin and distribution of this species suggests that the primary centre of origin of the cultivated apple is determined as the mountainous regions of the central Asia, the domestication of *M. sieverii* is held to be ancestor of the cultivated apple. The secondary centre of origin in which new intraspecific and interspecific has arisen in North America. (Ponomarernko, 1980).

The *M. sylvestris* (*M. praecox*) *M. orientalis* and *M. siversii* (includes *M. niedzwetzkyang*), *M. domestica* is treated as a complex hybrid derived from *M. orientalis* and *M. siversii* (Silbereisen, 1985).

Important cultivars

Ambri

It is only indigenous variety grown in Kashmir, fruits are medium large, oblong shape red streaks over greenish yellow background and late. Excellent keeping quality 4-5 month ordinary condition and 10 months cold storage.

Red Delicious

The fruits are large, oblong, conical covered with red streaks on a pale background. Flesh creamy white, tender crisp, fruits matures 133-139 days from full bloom.

Golden Delicious

The trees are moderately vigour, medium to large fruit, oblong, skin golden, yellow, with russetted prominent small dots scattered all over. Flesh creamy white , fine crip, sweet. It is a good pollinizer for all the delicious group. It requires 148-159 days from full bloom to maturity.

Starking Delicious

Fruit oblong conic with red strips, juicy, and sweet in taste. It require 115-120 days from bloom to maturity, it is budsport of red delicious.

Versifield

(Mahraji) It is widely grown in Kashmir valley. It is called Mahraji probably because the earlier trees were grown in Kashmir maharaja garden. Trees in vigourous and prolific bearing habit,bienniceal bearing habit. Fruit matures in October large sized flat in shape with red strips, white dots prominently found, hence also called as white dotted red.

Rich-e-Red

It is also bud sport of Red Delicious, conical in shape, skin red blush, colour earlier than Red delicious but later than Stranking Delicious. It is more completely coloured than Starking Delicious.

Vance Delicious

It is mutant of Red Delicious, outstanding variety, great demand by grower, conical in shape, solid colour, colour at least weeks earlier to Red Delicious and hence, sold at premimum price.

Baldwin

An American variety, very successful in Kullu Valley, fruit are of large sized, deep bright red colour; flesh yellowish white, crispy, juicy, tender.

Cox Orange Pippin

Fruit medium sized, round, oblate, symmetrical, skin orange red deepening to bright red flesh, yellow, firm, crip, tender, very juicy, oromatic, best dessert apple. A regular and heavy bearer variety.

New apple hybrids

Lal Ambri

It is progeny of Ambri and Red Delicious; it was released in 1973-74, average yield 35-40 mt/ ha, mature last week of September, high quality and high yielding.

Sunehari

A hybrid of Ambri and Golden Delicious; released in 1973-74, high quality over Golden Delicious, mature in September, average yield 64-72 kg/per tree.

Shireen

(Lord lambourne x Melba x R 12740-7A). This variety was released in 1995, moderately vigour tree, regular oval to conical in shape, greenish yellow background. Colour with red orange blush dominating 2/3 of fruit, fruit matures 139-144 days from date of bloom, yield 32-40kg per tree scab resistant, field resistant to alternaria, leafspot, and powdery muldew.

Firdous (Golden delicious X Rome Beauty X *M. floriburda*)

It was released in 1995, moderately vigours tree, upright, spreading open, spur and top bearer, fruit yellow colour of ground, bright red blushed. Takes 119-122 days after full bloom.

Chaubattia Anupam

A hybrid of Early Shannbury and Red Delicious, released from Horticulture Experiment Training Centre, Chaubattia, Almora, Uttranchal. Tree with moderate vigour, very sweet, matures in the end of june.

Chaubattia Princess

(Early Shannbury and Red Delicious). It was also released from H. E. T. C. Chautbattia, Uttaranchal, tree with moderate vigour, very sweet and free from scab disease.

Both varieties viz. Chaubattia Anupam and Chaubattia Princess were evolved by Seth and Ghildyal, (1984).

Ambred

(Red Delicious x Ambri)- Tree is tall, spreading and open, fruits are medium in size, conical, symmetrical shape with bright red strips, flesh whitish, crisp, firm, aromatic and juicy, fruit matures in September. It shows low incidence of powdery mildew, sooty blotch and scab.

Ambstarking (Starking Delicious x Ambri)

Tree vigours, tall and open fruit is medium in size, round conical and symmetrical, uniform shape. Dots are numerous and conspious. The plants are tolerant to scab disease.

Systematic description of pear

The cultrivated pears derived from two sources European and the Oriental pear. The pear belongs to genus *Pyrus* it differs from genus *Malus* in presence of grit cells.

The tree develops large size upright growing habit, producing thorn- like leafy spurs, the young growth becoming glabrous, leaves oval to oblong; ovate hard texture, smooth, bright colour, with prominent short point, serratures fine, flower white or rarely tirged pink, one inch or more across 4 to 12 together on slender pedicels, appearing with first foliage, fruit mostly pyriform in shape with tapering base. Sometimes apple shaped (pomiform).

Important Species of *Pyrus*

P. communis-Common cultivated pear/French pear/ Occidental pear/ English pear

P. sinensis **Chinese** (Sandpear).

P. serotino, P. pyrifolia. L. **Oriental pear/ Japanese pear**

Snow pear *P. nivalis*

Pyrus communis L(European pear or common pear)

It is occasionally thorny, deciduous tree with ovate to elliptic glossy, dark green leaves to 10cm long, with fine forward pointing teeth. Flowers are white in colour, often tinged pink in bud are borne in umbel like recemes of 5-9 in mid- spring, fleshy pedicel and pyriform fruit.

P. pyrifalia (Burm F.) or *P. serotiria*. var. Culta (Chinese or sand pear or Japanese pear)

Trees are 8-10 m in height, having spreading habit of growth, dark light brown in colour with presence of lenticels. Bark surface rough and splitting, branches are drooping type, pubescence present on young shoots leaves mostly ovate, 10-15 cm long, margin crenate, base round, apex narrowly acuminate, leaves are dark green above and light green below, mid-rib pale green. Calyx are deciduous in nature pedicel non-fleshy, and fruit shape apple like pomiform.

***P. jacquimontiana* Dcne. Jard**

It is locally known as 'Besar', the trees are open headed, bears small roundish to oblong and brownish colour fruits with numerous raised lenticels.

***P. pashia.* Hamilton.(Kainth)**

Kainth is mainly used for raising of rootstocks. Trees are having upright growing habit (19m height). Branches are thicker, leaves elliptical, margins serrated, leaf base and apex acute 5-7cm long. This species is found from the Himalayas to Northern China. The trees are vigorous, bear small round gritty fruits of very poor quality. It is used as root stock and is a very vigours.

***P. serotina* Rehd. (Shiara)**

It is wild grown species of pear mainly used as root stock, trees are 8-9 m in height, spreading in nature leaves ovate, 8-10 cm long, pointed at the tip, medium in size, spines are long stout and pointed, leaf margin finely serrated, deciduous calyx and apple like shape of fruit. *Purus serotina* Rehd.var. culta is a Japanese pear.

P. calleryana

Tree broadly conical shape, very thorny generally, deciduous tree with ovate to broadely ovate finally scalloped or toothed, glossy, dark green leaves, white flower, umbel like inflorescence, spherical, brown fruits. It appears to be resistant to phytophtora root rot, owk root fungus and crown gall.

***P. polycarpa* Hook. F.**

It grows wild in Shillong and Somarin area of Meghalaya. Fruits small globose in cluster good root stock. It is free from powdery mildew and fire blight.

***P. nivalis* (Snowpear)**

Broad conical shape, thornless deciduous tree with

elliptic to ovate, entire or shallowly scalloped silvery grey leaf. It bears white flower, umbel like raceme inflorescence, yellow green fruit.

P. salicifolia

Tree spreading and deciduous, pendent shoots and lance shaped to narrowly elliptic grey-felted leaves, creamy white flower, umbel like inflorescence, 6-8 in number.

P. ussuriensis

Trees are of broadly conical deciduous tree with broadly oval, glossy, dark green leaves, white flower are borne in umber racemose inflorescence.

Origin of Pear

European cultivated varities are found to be possess feature characteristics of *P. Caucasica P. elaeagnifolia, P. nivalis, P. Pyraster, P. salicifolia and P. syriaca* which are thought to be most likely progenitors of the cultivated pears. It is supposed that the primary assortment of European pear varities originated in the Caucasus on the basis of interspecific hybridization (Tuz, 1978). *P. cordata found* in Western Europe should be regarded as separate species, related not to *P. pyraster* but to *P. Magyarica* (Sec *Pashia)* found in Hungary, majority of wild pear population found in the Balkan Peninsula, which have pubescent, narrow obovate, leaves oblong to *P. Slavonica rather* than *P. elaeagrifolia* or *P. Nivalis* (Terpo, 1985).

Important cultivars

William Bartlette

It was originated from England, most popular commercial cultivar all over world. The tree is prolific, heavy and regular bearer, fruits are medium to large in size, ovate pyriform green when picked, turning bright yellow on ripening.

Max Red Bartlette

It is bud sport of Bartlette, the tree and fruit character are resemble to parent except fruit skin which are dark cran berry red colour. Tree tall, spreading productive and short, fruits mature later than Bartlette.

Starkrimson Delicious

It is an all over red bud sport, fruits are large in size, and most perfectly flavoured pears, fruit texture tender, fine grained and buttery, no grit cells, fruits are brilliant red colour when ripe.

Baghu Gosha

It is commercially being cultivated in Kashmir Valley, fruit medium, round or conical skin greenish yellow with russet patches, flesh, greenish white, firm and juicy, moderately sweet flavoured.

Conference

Fruits are of medium sized, pyriform shape, skin green with russet patches, sweet juicy, flesh, regular cropper and good bearer.

Anjou

It is most important pear cultivar after Bartlette. The tree comes into bearing late but regular bearing habit. The fruit is large, bright green, turning greenish-yellow when ripe. It had excellent keeping quality can be stored 8 months at 1^0 c temperature.

Flemish Beauty

The trees are spreading and high yielder, fruit large, ovate, smooth and attractive, flesh clean, white, very juicy almost free from grit cells with sweet aromatic flavour and high keeping quality. It is self fertile and good pollinizer.

Vicar of Wink Field

A medium to vigorous tree fruits are of extra large size pyriform shape mature late, excellent keeping quality yellow colour skin with whitish flesh.

Low chilling pear-

Kieffer

The tree is vigorous productive, self fruitful, medium to large fruit, brownish gritty and hard flesh, suitable for processing.

Gola

Grown in low hills prolific bearer cultivar fruit roundish with excellent shipping quality.

Le-Conte

It is low chill cultivar, can be grown in low to mid hills. The fruit is of medium growth heavy bearer. The fruit is small round and yellowish green.

Pathernakh

It is also low chill cultivar which is grown in submountaneous areas. It can stand high temperature hot winds and water logging and drought. The tree heavy yielder, fruits are medium in size with prominent dots, the flesh is juicy, crispy and gritty, skin very tough hence resist well to rough handling.

Peach (*Pyrunus persica* (L.) Batsch

Peach *P. persica* and *P. amygdalus* have somatic number 16, they have a number of common characteristics including both graft and pollen compatibility. Branched taproot system, aerial erect branched, cylindrical, solid woody, special dwarf shoots, flower borne from one year old shoot, the branch which had bear fruit for one time become barron. Leaves oblong, lanceolate to broad lanceolate 10-12 cm long exstipulated, sub-sessile, with many pair of glands at the base of each leaf, alternate simple toothed finely, sharp serrate when young otherwise coarsely serrate and glabrous leaf.

Flowers are solitary or in cymose cluster at the tip of shoot simple perfect complete perigyrous, flower sub sessile or pedicellate, complete actinomorphic thalamus cup-shaped, pentamerous, pink appearing before leaf emergence, sepals 5 gamosepalous, calyx tube companulate, caducous, green woody petals 5, polypetalous, pink, imbricate stamens many (10-60), polyandrous, inserted at the ridge of calyx tube, anther dehisced longitudinally, carpel one superior, unilocular placentation, marginal ovule-2, simple style and stigma capitate.

Fruit widely variable in size and shape, velvety skin with yellow dark red colour, flesh white or yellow, stone very hard and deeply pitted or furrowed seed may be free, semi clinging or clinging type with flesh. Seed non-endospermic.

Clinging stone- seed cling to flesh at ripening e.g. Sharbati.

Free stone- seeds are easily separated at ripening e.g. Floridasun, Elbertta, generally free stone varieties are preferred for canning purpose because seeds are separated easily.

Nectarine- *P. persica* var. Nucipersica) It is group of peach with recessive gene which results in fuzzless fruit, important cultivars are Legrand, Sunlite, SunRed, Sunrise, Sunripe, Nectared and Red Nectarine (Red Gold).

Important species.

P. davidiana - Broadly upright tree, deciduous, dark green leaves long bronze red when young, bowl shape, pink flower, spherical woody yellow fruit.

P. fergamensis

P. kansuensis

P. behmi
P. mira

It is natural hybrid of almond and peach, this species occurs extensively in the dry temperate zone of Kinnaur Himachal Pradesh.

P. besseyi- It is used as dwarfing rootstocks.

P. mira.

Low Chilling Cultivars.

Sharbati

It was selected from HETC, Saharanpur, fruit is full of juice and fruits are available in mid June.

Safeda Early Cream

Florida Sun

Florida Red

Florida Bell

Florida Gold

Florida King

Florida Queen

Shane-e-Punjab, Safeda, Saharanpur Prabhat, South Land

High Chilling Varieties

Stark Early Flame

Alexander

Peregreen

Elbertta- world leading variety.

Quetta Saharanpuri

July Elbertta

Candor

Craw Ford Early

Golden Bush

J.H. Hale
Babcock (Strawberry Peento)
Dixigem
Early Amber.

Plum

Plums are most important stone fruits, belongs to genus *Prunus* of the sub family, Prunoidae of the Rosaceae family. Plum are related species have been placed in the subgenus *Prunophora,* section *Euprunus* and *Prunocerasus* (Knight. 1969). Watkins (1976) views that *P. salicina* of China as the link between the sections *Prunocerasus* and *Euprunus.*

Prunus domestica (European plum) is believed to be the most recent species have arisen within the section *Prunophora, P. insititia, P. cerasus* and *P. spinosa* are thought to be involved in evolution of *P. domestica* (Endlich and Murawski, 1962; Watkins, 1976; Salesses, 1977).

P. domestica- it was arose by somatic doubling of sterile triploid hybrid of *P. cerasifera,* (2n=16) and *P. spinosa* (2n-32). European plum is a large tree 30-40 feet in height with thick twigs, pubescent when young smooth tree bark, leaves thick, glossy dull green above and pale green underneath, leaves large, ovate or abovate, shoot pointed to obtuse, coarsely and irregularly serrated, margin notched, flower may be solitary or in umbel like inflorescence, flower white or cream in colour mostly clustered on spures but sometimes single or 2 or 3 together, pedicles mostly pubescent. Fruit variable and variously coloured, often blue-purple, usually ovoid to oblong fruit.

P. salicina- (Japanese plum)- It was originated in China. It was introduced into Japan some 200-400 years ago, from where it got disseminated around the world, hence, known as Japanese Plum. It is small growing tree, the species is more vigorous, productive, precocious and more resistant to disease, leaves oblong, obovate or oblong ovate, not prominent by rugose, usually shinning above, prominently pointed closely blunt serrate, dull and usually glabrous beneath. Flower produced in a cluster of 3 in a bud, on the spurs pedicel glabrous and slender. The fruit set is heavier and more consistent on spur. The fruits are usually large and heart shaped often with a pronounced apex, which differ it from another plum species.

Other species

P. spinosa (The black thorn sloe)

P. cerasifera (Myrobalan Plum)

P. ussuriensis (Ussurian plum)

P. nigra (Canada Plum)

P. americana (American plum)

P. insititia (small fruited, European plum)

P. cerasifera sub sp. Orientalis (Orientalis Myrobalan plum (Luneva, 1984)

P. curatillifolia (Mobola plum)

P. excelsa Guinea plum)

P. capensis

P. compestris

P. nonda

Important cultivars

Prune

Prune is a group of European plum variety having high chilling requirement. Fruit contain high TSS and low moisture, hence they are ideally suitable for dehydration purpose. This is commercially most important group in the Eastern world, fruits are blue or purple in colour, flesh is firm and thick. All pruns are plum but all plums are not prunes. Important cultivars Italian Prune, Sugar Prune, Giant Prune, Agen Prune, Fresh Prune, Jefferson, President,

Green Gage

The fruit is medium in size, roundish with greenish yellow skin, flesh is firm, free stones with good flavour, flesh Reine Claude- It had an exquisite flavour, tree is compact, self sterile and blooms very late, fruit is large, orange in colour and speckled.

White Victoria

It is most widely grown cultivar of all the European varieties. The tree is very vigorous and self-fertile, prolific bearer and frost resistant.

Starking Delicious

Fruit medium with dark red skin and blood red flesh colour with good fruit quality.

Early Transparent Gage

Regular, heavy and prolific bearer, fruit small and roundish.

Golden Transparent

It is dwarf in nature, self- fertile bloom late, fruit is very delicious.

Dennistons Superb

This is not true Reine Claude Plum, but a hybrid, it possess true gage flavour, extremely hardy and fertile. It is good pollinizer for many other cultivars.

Golden Drop– (Yellow egg plum)

It blooms early, requires frost protection, large fruit, with peculiar flavour. The fruit has rich apricot flavour and characteristics sweetness.

Japanese Cultivars

Santa Rosa

It is complex hybrid of *P. salicina, P. simonii, and P. americana.* The tree upright growth habit, it is commercial grown cultivars in Kashmir valley, large fruit with a red – crimson colour. The flesh is umber but red near the skin. It is self fruitful, a prolific bearer and had characteristic flavour. The drawback is of soft watery flesh and sourness near pit.

Beauty

This is also self-fruitful cultivars, heart shaped, greenish yellow to bright crimson and the flesh is amber streaked with scarlet.

Mariposa

The tree upright growing habit. It require cross pollination for good set. The fruit is heart-shaped with greenish yellow skin with red flesh.

Other cultivars are Alubukhara, Aloocha, Titron, Jamuni, First Plum, China Plum, New plum, Maynard, Ramgarh Maynard, Methley, Kelsey, etc.

Hybrids of *P. spinosa*

P. x barboensis (P. elaeagrifolia x P. spinosa)

P. x velenovskyi (P. pyraster x P. sinosa)

P. x jordanovii (P. communis x P. sinosa)

Apricot - *Prunus armeniaca*

Apricot had no low chiling cultivars, its cultivation on lower valley is not possible and altitude. Important cultivars are as follows

- Turkey
- Conian Italy
- Shipley Early

- New Castle
- Castle Bright
- Charmagz
- Orgrand
- Alba
- Kaisha
- Halman
- Rakcha Karpu

Hybrids

- Chaubattia Alankar - Kaisha x Charmagz
- Chaubattia Madhu - Turkey x Charmagz
- Chaubattia Kesri - St. Ambriose x Charmagz

Chapter 17

Systematic Description of Tree Nuts

Walnut

Phylum - Angiospermae

Sub phylum - Dicotyledons

Division - Lignosae

Order - Juglandales

Family - Juglandaceae

Genus - *Juglans*

Systematic position of family juglandaceae according to Taxonomist

Hutchinson	**Bentham and Hooker**
Phylum - Angiospermae	Group - Angiospesms
Subphylum - Dicotyledones	Sub groups-Dicotyledon
Division - Lignasae	Division - Monochlamydae
Order - Juglandales	Series - Unisexuales
Family - Juglandaceae	Family - Juglandaceae

Engler and Prantle

Angiospermae

Class - Dicotyledoneae

Sub class- Archichlamydeae (Apetalae)

Order - Juglandales

Family - Juglandaceae

Salient Feature of Genus *Juglans*

i) The trees are large deciduous and monoecious plants with large pinnately leaf compound. The bark strong scented, hollow branches divided into small chamber.

ii) It bears staminate of flowers in long pendulous catkins found on one year old shoot.

iii) The pistillate flowers are small and borne one terminal racemes on current season wood.

iv) The fruit is a nut with slight to deep furrow, roughened nut, enclosed in a thick indehiscent husk or finally separating into two halves. The seeds are lobed and fit into shell, packed with tissues.

Important *Guglans* Species

Juglans ailanthifolia Cart. (Heart nut or Siebold nut) syn – *J. sieboldiana* (Maxim), *J. mirabunda* (Koidz.), *J. laballei* (Dode.), *J. coarctata* (Dode).

Tall erect tree up to 20m tall, branches grayish brown, densely glandular and pubescent when young. Leaves large, petiole with 9 to 21 leaflets, leaflets ovate - oblong, 8 -12 cm long, apex acute to acuminate abruptly, staminate 10 to 20 cm long, pistillate aments 10 to 30 flowered, fruits are borne in long raceme and in good locations, tree produce prolifically, after maturity nut starts falling on ground, nut pubescent with hard shell, broadely avoid to nearly globose 2.5 to 3.5 cm long, raised sutures.

J. californica Wats. (California Black walnut)

It is a type of shrub or tree in nature, branching occur from the ground, forming a wide, spreading tree than height. Leaflets are 1.25 to 2.50 inches long. It had tendency to produce abundantly sucker at the crown which is an undesirable characteristics of the California black walnut. Staminate flowers slender 5-7cm long, brownish and pubescent, calyx labe acute, stamens 30–40 in number.

Pistillate flower in cluster, ovoid with recurved yellow stigma, 10–12mm long.

Nut fruits are globose in shape of 20–30 mm in diameter with thin dark brown soft pubescent husk, thin walled nut.

J. hindsii Jeps. (California or Hinds blade walnut) Deciduous round - topped tree 10 - 20 m tall, occasionally 25m with erect unbranched trunk 3 - 13 m, 30 - 60 cm in diameter. Bark strong scented, gray brown smooth leaves 22-30cm long, alternate compound leaf ovate - lanceolate to lanceolate long pointed, serrate margin, base rounded cuneate to cordate, lower leaf surface with tuft of hours, staminate flower in slender, glabrous 7.5 -13 cm long, calyx elongated, covered with pubescence, 5 or 6 lobed, stamens 30 to 40, pistillate flowers oblong–ovoid, thickly covered with villose pubescent.

Fruit subglobose 3–5 cm across, soft pubescent, nut nearly globose, thick shelled seed small and sweet.

This species generally planted as a avenue tree and most widely used as root stocks for Persian walnut. North America is considered as centre of diversity. Fruits and timbers are valuable product.

J. nigra L (Eastern Black walnut) - A tall erect tree upto 150 feet height, long lived (100 years) old trees, straight trunk, often unbranched up to 20 m, 1.3 to 2 m in diameter, branches forming a round topped, mostly upright and rigid, twigs light brown with channeled pith, terminal buds as broad as long. The bark is characteristically deep furrowed, rough with numerous narrow ridges. The other characteristics feature is that it remain dormant for long when other walnut species are full in leaves. Further, it is one species which drop leaves earliest in the fall season. Leaves compound deciduous, 30-60 long petiole pubescent, with 13 to 23 leaflets, leaflets 7.5 to 8 cm long, 2.5 to 3 cm wide, long pointed, sharply serrated slightly rounded at base.

Staminate catkins are 5-10 cm long, brackets are triangular usually brown and hairy, stamens are 20-30 in many series, nearly sessile. Pistillate flowers 2-5, flowered spike, bract with pale glandular hair, calyx-lobe ovate, acute.

Fruit solitary or in pair, globose oblong and slightly pear shaped or pointed at apex, husk yellow green, or green smooth. Fruit large in size, 3.5 to 5 cm across. The nuts with thick shell marked on the surface with deep narrow furrows and irregular ridges. The nuts are brown to nearly black in colour after drying.

J. cinerea Linn (Butter nut or white walnut or oil nut)

Trees of 35 m height, straight trunk of 0.6 to 1m in diameter, round topped, bark smooth, light gray on young branches, becoming light brown and deeply fissured bark, widely spreading branches and light brown wood. This species is easily identified by its long, ovoid–oblong nuts with 4 prominent and 4 less prominent sharp irregular ridges and a very thick shell. Fruits in drooping cluster.

Leaves 35 to 7cm long with stout pubescent petioles, compound with 11 to 17 oblong. Laneolate leaflets 5 to 7.5 cm long. Finely serrated glandular sticky. Leaf scars are also characteristics, having a cushion of hair above the leaf scar, and stems having pointed terminal buds on the twigs.

J. regia L. (English Walnut or Persian Walnut)

It is valued as an orchard tree for commercial nut production. Nuts are consumed fresh. It is deciduous manoecious tree of 12-15 m tall, or rarely up to 60 m tall, bark brown or gray, smooth, fissured, leaf scar prominent leaves alternate, pinnate without stipules, leaflets 15 to 24 opposite, 6-12 cm long, ovate-oblong to ovate lanceolate, acuminate, margin irregular, serrate.

Flower developing from dormant buds of previous seasons growth, staminate flower catkins 5-10 cm length in axillary position, each catkins having 1 to 4 million pollen grains perianth segments 1 to 4, stamens 3-4 in numbers.

Pistillate flowers occurs in single, two or three in terminal raceme on new wood (current season growth) style divided into two plumose stigma perianth 4 lobed. Fruit 3.5 to 5 cm in diameter, globose or single obvoid, nut ovoid, acute, strongly ridged not splitting, green hulled of 3-10 cm across. Some varieties are having thick shelled some with soft (paper) shelled.

Walnut Hybrid

Royal - It is a progeny of *J. nigra* x *J. hindsii*, was developed by Luther Burbank, it is reported to be an extremely vigorous grower.

Paradox - Hybrid of *J. hindsii x J. regia*.

Classification of Walnut species

Section A. Dioscaryon. White walnut trees belong to this section e.g *J. regia.*

Section B. Rhysocaryon - Black walnut trees.

Section C. Trachcyaryon - Butternut, these species are found in Eastern United States e.g. *J. cinerea.*

Section D. Cardiocaryon - Japanese walnut trees heart nut belong to this species.

e.g. *J. ailanthifola, J. cathayensis, J. mandshurica* etc.

Other species of walnut

J. australis

J. boliviana

J. californica

J. hindsii

J. hissuta

J. jamaicensis

J. major

J. mollis

J. neotropica

J. olanchana

J. pyriformis

J. soratensis

J. steyermarkii

J. venezuelensis

J. cathayensis

J. mandshurica

Important Cultivars of Walnut

Hartley

It is one of the most popular commercial cultivar of California, its desirable traits are light kernel colour and good yield. It require congenial cultural condition for its potential yield.

Payne

It is another important cultivars of California. It had high yield potential due to fruitfulness of lateral buds. This cultivar can be grown in solid block because pollen and stigma mature simultaneously.

Franquette

It is an old and leading cultivar of France. It escape late spring frost, because late bud break take place. It is harvested about a week later than other cultivars. Nuts are small in size with good seal and light kernel colour.

Ashley

It is high yielding cultivars being fruitful up to 90% on lateral buds and consequently requires heavy pruning to keep the tree vigorous. Nuts are ovoid in shape gives about 54% kernel yield of good quality.

Hamdaan, it was released from SKUAST-K Srinagar. Trees are of somewhat dwarf, spreading, having 7 leaflets. The leaflets are elliptical, serrated and light green in colour. It is very precocious and bearing starts 3-5 years after planting. Nut weight of 11.70g, with 8.05g kernel weight and extra light colour with 54.76% shelling.

Sulaiman

This was also selected from seedling population by SKUAST-K, Shalimar, Srinagar. Sulaiman had average nut weight 21.50g light colour kernel, kernel weight 11.26g, moderate filling nut, and 52.37% shelling, yield per tree after 5 years of age 30kg. There are huge demand of these cultivars in Kashmir valley.

Lake English

It is semi hard shelled with medium sized nut. Nut is dull white, with light brown kernel. After maturity, nut get easily separated from green hull. Its filling and taste are very promising.

Tuttle 16

Trees are large and bears regularly, nuts are large in size, white and well filled sweet kernel taste.

Tuttle 31

Trees are very large and productive. Nuts are large in size with dull in colour white and filling is very good, excellent kernel taste.

Kashmir Division witness wide range of variability as such 99 percent plantations are seedling origion every tree is a genotype itself. During the survey selection 60-70 promising selections made and collected at SKUAST-K, Srinagar Farm. Some most promising selections are SKUAW 0008, SKAUAW 0009, SKUAW 0010, SKUAW 0020 and SKUAW 0021, further survey process is going on.

Bearing Habit

Seedling trees have long juvenile phase (10-12 years) however, grafted walnut plants took 5-6 years for coming in fruit. It is monoecious plant of staminate and pistillate flowers are borne separately on the same tree. Staminate flowers emerge laterally on the previous season's growth and hang in catkins. Pistillate flowers appear in pairs in the form of nut lets at the tip of the current season's growth. The fruit bud formation of pistillate flowers, initiated during summer, yet its final development occurs shortly before anthesis in the following spring.

Walnuts are self-fruitful and cross compatible variety. Dichogamy also found, when flower do not shed pollen grain even after stigma is receptive. The most common type of dichogamy is protandry, but some protogyny also found. Nut starts growing when pollen tube starts growing on stigma, during first 2-3 weeks after pollination. Interestingly, pollinated and unpollinated flower grow at similar rate but non pollinated flower fall of at the end of 2-3 weeks.

Failure of fertilization is another form of flower drop, female shriveled and drop off shortly. This type of drop is known as pistillate flower abortion (PFA). This PFA is related to excess of pollen grain on stigma.

Pecans (Pecan nut)

Characteristic feature of Genus - (*Carya*) - Taxonomist recognizes 20 species of pecan and hickories. The trees of this genus are prized for their edible nuts which are of commercial importance. The accepted name of *Carya illinoensis* Wag. The pecan is largely self fertile but dichogamous. There are some cultivars of pecan in which male flower do not shed pollen at the time of stigma receptivity.

Salient features of important species

C. illinoensis Wagenheim

1. Large tree growing height about 100 feet deciduous in nature.
2. Strong and tough wood with smooth gray bark on young trees as it advances in age becoming rough with solid branches. Leaves alternate, pinnately odd or imparipinnate, oblong and lanceolated leaves.
3. Pecan being monoecious trees, staminate flowers are borne on pendulous tree branched catkin which may be solitary in leaf axils or on two years old branch, calyx 2-3 lobed and the stamens are arranged in 2 or 3 series. Pistillate flowers are borne terminally on the current growth in 2-8 flowered spikes with 4 lobed involucres enclosing a 1-celled ovary in it. Due to terminal bearing habit, it bears poorly.

The fruits are oblong to globular in shape, having a thick husk which separate in segments. The hulls are ridged. The nuts are smooth brown striped or complete brown in colour. The shell is very thin to moderate thick.

***C. ovata* (Mill) K. Koch-** It is also known as Shagbark Hickery, trees are large in size (90 feet height) with gray bark soon splitting into long and loosening plates. Branches scurfy-pubescent initially are becoming glabrous later, leaflets 5 or 7 elliptical. Staminate with 4-6 stamens. Fruits are subglobose to broadly aboviod, generally ovate, slightly flattered and angled thin shell and sweet kernel.

***C. laciniose* (Michx. F.) Loud-** It is also known as shell bark Hickory or Kingnut. This differ from Shaghbark hickory in having stouter and less pointed over wintering buds. The tree trunk is covered with flaps or folds from loosening plate of bark. Leaflets 7-9 oblong to lancolate, acuminate apex and pubescent below portion of leaves. Fruits are globose to obovoid, 4-7 cm long, nut subglobose or ellipsoid, pointed at the thick shell, with sweet kernel.

C. *myristicaeformis* Nutt. (Nutmeg Hickory) . It had ornamental view, can be used as ornamental plants.

C. *aquatica*- (Bitter pecan or Water Hickory)

C. *cordiformis* K. Koch (Pignut or Swamp Hickory)

C. *ovalis* Sarg. (Sweet Pignut or False Shagbeaf)

C. *glabra* (Smooth Pignut)

C. *pallida* Engl (Pale Hickory)

C. *tomentosa* (Mockernut or White Heart Hickory)

Chapter **18**

Systematic Description of Hazelnut (Virin)

Classification

Division – Phanerogams

Class- Angiosperms

Sub class- Dictotyledonea

Order- Fagales

Genus- Betulaceae (Corylaceae)

Genus- *Corylus*

The hazelnut has various synonyms such as Filbert, Cobnut, Barcelona nut, European hazel etc. After the hybridization and selection two main group emerged i.e. Filberts and Cobnuts. The filberts are long normal like human nail and the cobnuts are roundish and somewhat flattened.

The member of genus *Corylus* are perennial deciduous shrubs or small trees, native to north temperate zone with slender round zig-zag twigs. Trees are monoecious in nature. It bears filbert tree bears ovoid to globose buds. The staminate flower known as catkins borne in early winter Aug – September in Kashmir condition, catkins are in drooping position. Fruits are small in size $1/4^{th}$ inch long and with alternate toothed ovate leaves and a terminal bud. The pistillate flowers are head like and enclosed in a small scaly bud with 3-5 red or pink styles, protruding outwards. The fruits are an ovoid surrounded by leafy tubular involucres.

Important species of Hazelnut

C. colurna - This species have central leader common trunk, trunk prominently found. In this, species husk toothed and fleshy (thicker) and forked deeply into lence - like lobed after drying the lobes curl back facilitating easy fall of nut. The husk contain one nut, the husk may joint more than one (husk in form of cluster) which gives an appearance of spiny cactus.

C. avellena:- This is world's best quality hazelnut and commercially cultivated nut. It is also known as European filberts. It readily crosses with many other species and developed large variations. The husk is short and flared up which allow the nut to fall easily on the ground.

C. maxima- This species had long husk a number of interspecific hybrid had developed due to cross between *C. maxima* and *C. avellana.*

C. tibetica- This species is native to Western China. It is shrubby in nature attain a height of 3-7m.

C. americana- Fruits are medium sized enclosed with husk that are usually twice the length of nuts. Trees are shrub type.

C. cornuta- It found in the east coast of the North America. This is a beaked filberts and is very winter hardy.

C. chinensis- Trees are tall growing upto 40 m and produce nut that have husk strongly constricts above the nut result difficult in removing.

C. sieboldiana- This is also known as Manchurian and Japanese filbert. It is shrubby in nature attaining height up to 3- 5 m the husk constrict into a tube above the nut.

C. jacquemontii- It is called as the Himalayan Filberts, considered as the variety of the *C. colurna.* The tree produce small thick-shelled nuts.

C. ferox- It is indigenous to the northern India, Sikkim and Nepal.

Barcelona, Butter, Ennis, Northampton Ana, Self Husker, Skinner, Red Filbert, Webb's Prize, White Filbert, Princess Royal, Daviana, Kentisheob, Pearson's Prolific.

The apetalous female flowers are produced on lateral buds on shoots or catkins peduncles. An inflorescence contain 4-16 flowers each of which consists of a air of stigmatic styles, joined at the base pollination takes place in the late January, but fertilization do not occurs of 4-6 months later. After pollination, pollen tubes grow to the base of the styles and remain there in the resting period till the ovary get matures.

Pistillate flowers which develop into nuts are usually borne in lateral and terminal buds the previous season's growth. The staminate flowers which produce pollen grain are borne in naked catkins on short stalks either laterally on the previous season's growth or terminally shoot spurs. Which may also bear leaf on fruit bud.

Chapter 19

Systematic Description of Kiwifruit

Classification

Phylum - Angiospermae

Sub-phylum- Dictoyledons

Division - Lignosae

Order -Theales

Family - Actinidiacea

Genus - Actinidia

Kiwifruit is most recent introduction to India, it is important crop plant in many parts of the world. The name kiwifruit is very recent origin. Chinese gooseberry was a name in common usages in New Zealand and else where until the first export of fruit to United States, this name was considered unsuitable, hence an exporting company coined the name **"kiwifruit"**. The name had given universal acceptance. Dunn (1911) in fruit major known of the genus recognized 2-4 species and total number of texa is 40, further Li (1952) described 36 species and the distinct taxa then numbered over 50 and Liang (1983) revised the genus and described over 50 species and 100 distinct taxa.

Species and forms of *Actinidia*

Actinidia chnensis- Planch var. Chinensis- This species comprise soft-haired kiwifruit. The flower bearing stems are short (4-5 cm long). The fruit is almost spherical with soft hair, often shed off at maturity. Fergusan, (1980) described different forms of *Actinidia.*

Form 1- *A. Chinensis* var *Chinensis* form a *chinensis.*

Form 2- *A. Chinensis* var *Chinensis* Form a *Jinggangsh* anensis C.F. Liang.

This form having branches and petiole being covered by a dense, rough tomentam which is persistent.

Form 3: *A. chinensis* var *chinensis* Form a *rofopulpa* C.F. Liang and R.H. Huang. Fruits are smaller in size with reddishinner pericarp.

A. chinensis Planch var *hispida* C.F. Liang.

This form comprise stiff haired kiwifruit, young shoots and most of the flowering branchlet are covered with long stiff hairs, the leaves are larger and petioles have long stiff hairs.

Form 4- *A. chinensis* var *hispida* form a *hispida*

This forms of cultivar is in cultivation throughout world. Hayward, Bruno and Monty belongs to this form.

Form 5 - *A. chinensis* var *hispida* Form a *chlorocarpa* C.F. Liang. The fruits shed off stiff hairs and become smooth when ripe.

Form 6: *A. chinensis* var *hispida* Form a *Longipila* C.F. Liang et R.Z. Wang leaves are more tomentose at beneath and bristles on the branch are longer.

A. chinensis Plach. var. *setosa* Li,. It is also known as spiny kiwifruit. The petioles and stamens are covered with dense rust coloured stiff spine hairs. Fruits are spherical to oblong in shape. This variety is mostly found in Taiwan.

Salient feature of Kiwifruit

The stems are weak and vine in nature, the kiwifruit can easily be separated into trunk, main branches forming the permanent framework of the vine. The main stem of the newly planted vine is very weak and flexible and require support and careful training. Shoots in the current season come from axillary buds on canes of the previous season's growth. The shoots are of two type terminating, the growing tip wither and die and are devoid of any terminal buds), the non terminating shoots remain growing throughout season and can reach 3-5 m in length. The young shoots are covered with large number of multicellular hairs older stems have rough peeling bark. A jelly like mucilage present in most part of the kiwifruit plant, the root and fresh stems are richest source. The leaves are large, upper surface had a high gloss the lower is covered with a felting of copious hairs with long petiole. Leaves are arranged on the axis spirally it may be clockwise or anticlockwise. The leaf size are affected hyposition on the vine, the leaves on very young shoots or vines are often large in size.

The kiwifruits are functional dioecious. Staminate flowers have reduced ovary residual style, pistillate flower appear complete but stamens produce non-viable pollen grain. Though dioecious is not absolutes some staminate plants may produce small fruit this indicate that development of hermaphrodite cultivar is possible.

The flowering shoots are emerged from the axillary buds on the canes of the previous season's growth. Some buds are vegetative which gives rise to vegetative and floral growth. Flowers are found on terminating as well as non-terminating shoots. The staminate flowers occur in the group of 3 or more at each axils the flower stalks are long. The flowers are actinomorphic, hypogynous, sometimes tetramerous but usually pentamerous. The larger pistillate flower may contain more perianth than staminate flower. The perianth can easily be distinguished into calyx and corolla.

Sepals usually five, sometimes 3 or 4 or more connate at base, ovate to oblong obtuse to acute at the apex. The flower is cup shaped with five petals, the petals are twice of the length, breadth of the sepals. They are broadly obovate, rounded at the tip. The petals are pure white but eventually turns to golden in colour.

In the staminate flower, the gynoecium is considerably smaller and no ovule develop. Stamens are present in staminate and pistillate flowers are hypogynous, free stamens arranged spirally. The filaments are long, slender and greenish white, generally much shorter in pistillate flower; attached dorsally, versatile anthers which are oblong, acute to obtuse at the apex. Dehiscence of anther slit longitudinally. Stamens in staminate and pistillate flowers are similar.

In pistillate flowers, numerous carpels are found (usually more than 30) fused to form syncarpous, superior ovary. Each carpels bears two rows of 10-20 unitegmic anatropous ovules attached to central axis. The central core of the ovary are termed as columella. There are as many styles as there are carpels and are free persistent, radiating. Styles are like tube shape with v shaped stigma. In pistillate flowers, the styles are generally small and rudimentary.

The fruit is a berry, glabrous or sometimes hairy and contain large number of seeds, the shape, size, external appearance of the kiwifruit is differ variety to variety and species to species. As per report, the fruit of *A. chinensis* var. chinensis is usually spherical with light brown, sparse, short and soft skin hairs. (Oliver, 1887, Liang, 1975, Anon, 1979). However, fruit of variety *hispida* is most attractive and elongated ovoid shaped, skin brown and densely covered with long stiff hairs. Fruit of variety *Setosa* is also covered with bristle- like hairs. Sepals of var. *hispida* are persistent but in var *chinensis* sepals are less persistent, sometimes are found to attached with fruit. The desiccated styles are persistent until harvest in var. *hispida* less extent in var. *chinensis*.

Actinidia species

A. arguta- (Sieb, et. Zuee) Planch. Ex Miq- It is very cold hardy species, the fruits are small, skin smooth, flesh is Juicy and fruit had very appealing flavour. This species ripens on the tree vine hence difficult to hardling or store.

A. kolomikta (Maxim. Et Rupr)- It is more cold hardy can withstand as low as 30⁰C temperature. Fruits are small but very sweet and has a fine aroma and flavour. It is having remarkably high content of vitamin C. this species grown as ornamental vine because of the striking pink and white to variegation younger leaves.

Achinidia chinensis- Have greater commercial potential than *A. deliciosa* about 1/3rd of all kiwifruit plantings in China are of *A. chinensis.* However, in New Zealand nearly 20% of all kiwifruit orchards are now planted in *A. chinensis.* The best known *Actinidia* species are *A. chinensis* and *A. deliciosa* but, these are only two genus comprise nearly 76 species and 125 taxa (Huang, *et. al* 2000 a, b) distributed in China and adjoining areas.

Liang, listed 51 species in China, 21 of which were further sub divided giving an additional 41 taxa. 35 varieties and 6 Forms.

Liang (1984) mentioned the taxa of *Actinidia.* Lindl. As described by Ferguson (2007).

A. *arguta* (Sieb et Zucc). Planch ex Miq

A. *arguta* var. Cordifolia (Miq.) Bean.

A. *arguta* var. *giraldii* (Diels) Voroshilov

A. *arguta* var *nervosa* C.F. Liang

A. *arguta* var *purpurea* (Rehder) C.F. Liang. Q.Q. Chang

A. *arisanensis* Hayata

A. *callosa* Lindl.

A. *arguta* var *acuminata*

A. arguta var *discolor*

A. arguta var *ephippioidea* C. F. Liang

A. arguta var *formosana* Finet et Gagnep

A. arguta var *henryi* Maxim

A. arguta var *pubiramula* C.F. Wu

A. arguta var *strigillosa* C.F. Liang

A. arguta var *carnosifolia* C.F. Wu

A. carnosifolia var *glaucescens* C.F. Liang

A. chengkouensis C.Y. Chang

A. Chinensis Planch

A. chinensis var *jinggangshanensis* C.F. Linang

C.F. Liang et. A. R. Ferguson.

A. chinensis var. *rufopulpa* (C.F. Liang et. R.H. Huang) C.F. Liang et A.R. Ferguson.

A. hemsleyana Dunn

A. hemsleyana var *Kengiana* (Metcalf) C.F. Liang

A. henanesis C.F. Liang

A. henryi Dunn

A. henryi var *glabricaulis* (C.F. Y Wu) C. F. Liang

A. henryi var *Polyodonta* Hand Mazz

A. holatricha Finet et Gagnep

A. hubeiensis H.M. Sun et R.H. Haung

A. Hypoleuca Nakai

A. indochinensis Merr

A. Jiangkouensis S.D. Shi et Z.S. Zhang

A. jiangxiensis

A. kolomikta (Maxim et Rupr.) Maxim

A. kolomikta var gagnepaini (Nakai) L.

A. laevissima C.F. Liang

A. laevissima var *floscula* S.D. Shi

A. *lanceolata* Dunn
A. *hemsleyana* var *latifolia* (Gardn. et Champ) Merr
A. *latifolia* var *mollis* (Dunn) Hand Muzz
A. *leptophylla* C.Y. Wu
A. *liangguangensis* C.F. Liang
A. *chrysantha* C.F. Liang
A. *cinerascens* C.F. Liang
A. *cinerascens* var longipetiolata C.F. Liang
A. *cinerascens var. tenuifolia* C.F. Liang
A. *cylindrica* C.F. Liang
A. *cylindrica* var *cylindrica F. obtusifolia* C.F.Liang
A. *cylindrical* var. *reticulate* C.F. Liang.
A. *deliciosa* (A. chev.) C.F.Liang et A.R. Farguson
A. *deliciosa* var *changanensis*
A. *deliciosa* var *chlorocarpa* (C.F.Liang) C.F.Liang et A.R. Ferguson.
A. *deliciosa*_var *coloris* T.H.Lin et X.Y. Xiong
A. *deliciosa* var l*ongipila* (C.F. Liang et R.Z.Wang) C.F. Liang et. A.R. Ferguson
A. *eriantha* var *brunnea* C.F. Liang
A. *eriantha* var. *calvescens* C.F.Liang
A. *lijiangensis* C.F. Liang et Y.X. Lu
A. *macrosperma* C.F.Liang
A. *macropserma* var *mumoides* C.F.Liang
A. *maloides* Li
A. *maloides* f. *cordata* C.F.Liang
A. *melanandra* French
A *melanandra"*var *cretacea* C.F.Liang
A. *melanandra* var *kwangsiensis* (Li) C.F.Liang
A. *melanandra subconcolo* C.F.Liang

A. melliana Hand Mazz
A. obovata Chun ex. C.F. Liang
A. persicina R.H. Huanget S.M. Wang
A. petelotii Diels
A. pilosula (Finet et Gagnep) staple ex Hand Mazz
A. polygama (Sieb at Zucc) Maxim
A. purpurea Rehder
A. rubricaulis Dunn
A. rubricaulis var *coriacea* (Finet et Gagnep) C.F.Liang
A. rubus H.Lev
A. rufa (Sieb et Zucc) Planch ex Mig.
A. fairchildii Rehder
A. fanjingshanensis S.D. Shi et Q.B. Wang
A. farinose C.F. Liang
A. fasiculoides C.F. Liang
A. fasiculoides var *orbiculata* C.F. Liang
A. fortunati Finet et Gagn
A. fulvicoma Hance
A. fulvicome var *lanata* (Hemsl) C.F. Liang
A. fulvicome f. hirsuta (Finet et Gagne) C.F. Liang
A. fulvicoma var *pachyhylla* (Dunn) L; Liang
A. gagnepaini Nakai
A. glauco- callosa C.F.Y Wu
A. glaucohylla F. Chun
A. glucohylla var. *asymmetrica* (F.Chun) C.F. Liang
A. glaucohylla var *robusta* C.F. Liang
A. globosa C.F. Liang
A. grandiflora C.F. Liang
A. rufotricha C.Y. Wu
A. sabiifolia Dunn

A. *setosa* (Li) C.F. Liang et A.R. Ferguson

A. *sorbiflora* C.F. Liang

A. *guilinensis* C.F. Liang

A. *stellato- pilosa* C.Y. Chang

A. *strigosa* Hook F. et Thoms

A. *styracifolia* C.F. Liang

A. *suberifolia* C.Y. Wu

A. *tetramera* Maxim

A. *tetramera var badongensis* C.F. Liang

A. *trichogyna* Franch

A. *truncatifolia* C.Y. Chang et .S. Liu

A. *ulmifolia* C.F. Liang

A. *ulmifolia* var. *Flabellifolia* C.F. Liang

A. *valvata* Dunn

A. *Valvata* var. *Boehmeriaefolia* C.F. Liang

A. *venosa* Rehder

A. *venosa f. pubescens* Li

A. *vitifolia* C.Y. Wu

A . *volubilis* sieb et Zucc

A. *zhejiangensis* C.F. Liang

Cultivars

Bruno - It pistillate cultivar, fruits are easily distinguishable from other cultivars by its slightly tapering shape towards the stem end. It is heavy bearer, average production and sweetness is more than other cultivar. Plant have less chilling requirement.

Allison - The fruits are medium in size and slightly tapering towards both ends, very much resembels to cv. Abbot, except that its fruits are slightly broarder in comparison to the length. It is heavy bearer cultivars.

Monty -It flowers late, fruits are oblong, medium size, slightly tapering, equally thick and flat at both ends, quite resembles with Allison and Abbott. Highly prolific bearer, require thinning.

Hayward - It is most popular variety, large fruit size, attractive oval shape, fruit is broad and flat, much wider than length. Fruits are barne singly at the nodes. This is comperatively shy bearer.

Tomuri - It is staminate cultivars, flowers usually appears in group of 5 late flowering. Good pollinizer for Hayward cultivars.

Abbott - Early flowering cultivar. Fruits are medium sized, covered with dense hairs, sweet in taste and low ascorbic acid content.

References

Bhatacharya, S.C. and Datta, S. (1951). Citrus variety of Assam. Indian J. Genet., 11 : 57-62.

Bhattacharya, S.C. and Datta, S.C (1956). A preliminary observation on root stocks for citrus in assam. Indian J. Hort., 9: 1-10.

Borges, T., Lima, H. and Febles, C. (1978). A cyto taxonomic investigation of C. medica L. Ciencias -Tecnicdlas.-Agricales. 1 (1): 5-47.

Brummitt, R.K. (1996). Quite happy with present code, thank you. In : J.L. Reveal (ed) Proc minisymposium on biological nomenclature in the 21st century. Univ. Maryland, Colleage Park w.w.w. inform. umd. edu./PBIO/nomcl/brum.html.

Cantino, P.D. and K. de,.Qusiroz (2000). Phlocode: A phylogenetic code of biological nomenclature http www. ohiou. edu/ phylocode/preface.html.

Citriculture, Rajput, CBS, Hari babu, R.S.Kalya (1997) Publishers New Delhi

Cronquist, A. (1968). the evoloution and classification of Flowering plants J.Nelson and Sons, London.

De Candolle, A.LP.P (1867). Loisde la nomenclature botanique. J.B. Billiera et fils. Paris.

De Queiroz, K., and Gauthur, J. (1992). Phylogenetic taxonomy. Annu Rev. Ecol. Syst., 23: 449-480.

De Queroz, K, and Gautheir, J. (1994). Toward a phyogenetic system of biological nomenclature. Trends Ecol u Evol, 9 : 27-31.

Dimitrov, S. (1980). New species from genus Malus Mill- apple. Nauchni- Trudors - vissh- Selskostoanski- Institut Vasil - Kolarov. 25 (4): 31-40.

Dostalek, J. (1984). Hybrid of Pyrus spinosa, Folia- Geobotanica -et- phyto taxonomica, 19 (1): 89-93.

Dunn, S.T. (1911). A revision of the genus Actinidia, Lindl I.Linn Soc. London, Bot. 39: 394-410.

Ferguson, A.R. (2007). Genetic resources of kiwifruit: Domestication and breeding. Horticultural Reviews, 33: 1-117.

Gilg, E. (1893). Dillenianceae, P. 100-128. in: H. [G.A]. Engler and K. [A.D.] Prantl (eds) Die naturlichen Pflanzenfamilien, nebst. ihrem Gattungen and Witchtigen Arten, insbesondere den Nutzflanzen.. Teil 3, Abt. 6, Lief 80. Verlag Wilhelm Engelmann, Leizig.

Greuter, W., Hawksworth, D.L. (from above reference (1997). Fourth draft Biocode: the perspective international rules for scientific names of organisms htt://www.rom.on.ca/biodiversity/ biocode 1997. html.

Greuter, W., Hawksworth, D.L.,McNeill, J.,Maya, M.A.,Minelli, A.,Sneath, P.H.A.,Tindoll, B.J., Trehane, P and Tubbs, P. (1996). Third draft Biocode: The prospective international rules for scientific names of organism. Taxon, 45: 349-372.

Greuter, W., Mc Neill, J., Barrie, F.R.,Burdett, H.M., Domoulin, V., Filgueiras, T.S., Nicolson, D.H., Silva, P.C., Skog, J.E., Trehane, P., Turland, N.J. and Hawksworth, D.L.(2002). (eds. And compilers). International Codes of Botanical Nomenclature (St Louis Code). Regnum Veg. 138:1-474.

Hanelt, P. (1986). Formal and informal classifications of the intraspecific variability of cultivated plants-advantage and limitations, p. 139-156. in: BT Styles (ed.) intraspecific classification of wild and cultivated plants, Clarendon Press. Oxford.

Hiwale, S.S. (2005). Goma Kirti : a new ber variety, Indian Hort., 50 (1): (24)

Huang, H.W., J.J. Gong , S.M. Wang, Z.C.He, Z.H., Zhag and J.Q.Li(2000b). Genetic diversity in the genus. Actinidia pp.65-79. In: H.W. Huang (ed.). Advances in Actinida Research, Science, Press, Beijing.

Huang, H.W., J.J.Gong, S.M.Wang, Z.C.He, Z.H.Zhag and J.Q.,Li (2000a). Genetic diversity in the genus Actinida. Chinese Biodiversity 8.,1-12.

Joshi, M.C. and Singh, S.M. (1980). New crab apple, Malus dirangensis from Arunachal Pradesh. Plant Science, 12 : 21-22.

Kapanadze, I.S. (1985). Citrus lapinii- a new hybrid species.

Soobscheniya- Akademii – nauk- Gruzinskoi- SSR. 120 (2): 389-392.

Karaya, R.K. (1987). Classification of pummelo and grape fruit (C paradisii Macf) Sbornik- Nauchnykh- Trudor-po- Prikladnoi-Botanike- Genetike- i- Selektsii, 112 : 62-69.

Kokaya, Ts.D. (1983). New taxa of the Junos type in the genus Citrus L. Trudy-po-Prikladnoi Botanike Genetike-i-Selektsii , 78: 95-103.

Korban, S.S. and Skirvin, R.M. (1984). Nomenclature of the cultivated apple. Hort. Science, 19. (2) : 177-180.

Kowatschew, I.G. and Kovachev, I. (1980). Two new species of the genus vitis L. from Bulgaria Feddes- Repertarium., 91 (1-2): 1-2.

Lapage, S.P., Sneath, P.H.A., Lessel, E.F., Sherman, V.B.D. Seeliger, H.P.R. and Clark, W.A.(1992) International Code of Nomenclature of Bacteria Published for the International Union of Microbiological societies by the Ame. Soc. Microbiology, Washington, D.C.

Lawerence, H.M. (1951). Taxonomy of vascular plants. Mcmillan New York.

Li, H.L. (1952). A taxonomic review of the genus Actinidia chinensis Planch (in Chinese). Acta Phytotaxon. Sin., 13: 32-35.

Liang, C.F. (1983). On the distribution of Actinidia as (in Chinese). Guihaia, 3 : 229-248.

Liang, C.F.(1984). Actinidia. p. 196-263, 309-324.In: K.M.Feng (ed). Flora Reipublication Popularis Sinicae, 49/2, Science Press, Beijing.

Luneva, N.N. (1984) The place of the oriental myrobalan plum in the system of the species Prunnus. Cerasifera Ehrh. Sbornik-Nauchnykh- Trudor-po-Prikladnoi-Botanike-Genetike-i.Selektsii, 88 : 106-108.

Mukherjee., S.K.(1949). A monograph on the genus Mangifera L. Lloydia., 12:73-136.

Mukherjee., S.K.(1985). Systematic and ecogeographic studies on crop gene pool: Mangifera L. International Board For Plant Genetic Resources Rome., Italy pp. 86.

Naqshi., A.R. (1993). An Introduction to Botanical nomenclature,

Scientific Publisher, Jodhpur.

Nath, Ravindra (1987). Plant Taxonomy ,Metropolitan Book Co. Pvt. Ltd. New Delhi.

Neill, J., Spongberg, S.A and Vrugtman, F. (1995). International code of nomenclature, of cultivated plants. Regnum Veg., 13:1-175.

Olmo, H.P. (1976). Grapes Vitis Muscadinia (Vitaceae). Evoloution of crop plants, (Ed. N.W.Simmonds), Wah Cheong Printing Press Ltd., Hong Kong, pp 294-298.

Panday, G. and Joshi, B.D. (1997). Kiwi : A Future fruits for the Indians Hills.

Ponomarenko, V.V. (1980). Current state of research on problems of the origin of M. domestica Borkh. Trudy- po-Prikladnai- Botanike Genetike-i-selektsii, 67 : 11-21.

Poyarkova, A.I. (1949). Actinidia Van Tiegh p. 138-147. in B.K. Shishkin (ed), Malvales, Parietales, Myrtiflorae, flora of USSR vol. XV. Translation of flora USSR XV. 185-197.

Ride, W.D., Cogger, H.G., Dupuis, C., Kraus, O. Minelli, A., Thompson, F.C. and Tubbs, P.K. (1999). International Code of Zoological Nomenclature 4th ed. Int. Trust for Zoological Nomenclature. Natural History Museum, London.

Scora, R.W.(1983). Chemical taxonomy of the genus citrus. Phytochemistry., 22 (1): 12.

Scora, R.W., Kumamota, J., Soost, R.K and Nauer, E.M.(1982). Contribution to the origin of grape fruit (C. paradisii). Systematic Botany, p 170-177.

Scrora, R.W., Nickolson, D.H.(1986). The current name for the Shaddock C. maxima not C. grandis. Taxon, 35 (3): 592-595.

Shreff, E.D. (1940). The delimitation of genera from the conservative point of view. Bull. Torrey bot. Club., 67: 375-380.

Shukla, Anil Kumar Shukla, Arun Kumar and Vashistha B.B. (2004). Fruit Breeding approaches and achievement. International Book Distributing Company Lucknow, U.P.

Shukla, Priti and Mishra, S.P.,(1979). An introduction to Taxonomy of Angiosperms,. Vikas publishing House Pvt. Ltd, New Delhi.

Silbereisen, R. (1985). Recent conceptions about the possible origin of the cultivars and rootstocks of Malus domestica Borkh. Acta Horticulturae. 139: 91.

Simmonds, N.W. and Shephered, K. (1955). The taxonomy and origin of the cultivated bananas. J. Linn. Soc., 55 : 302-312.

Sooner, D.M. (2003). Plant nomenclature and taxonomy. Horticultural Reviews, 28: 1-61

Spooner, D.M. and Berg van den, R.G. (2003). Plant nomenclature and Taxonomy : An Horticultural and Agronomic Perspective. Horticultural Reviews 28 : 2-60.

Srivastava, R.P., Pathak, R.K., Bana, D.S. and Pandey, V.S. (1977). Utilization of some important fruit trees growing wild in the Himalayan region. In : Fruit Breeding in India (Ed.) Nijjar, G.S. Oxford and IBH Publishing Company, New Delhi, pp. 1-8.

Stafleu, F.A (1971). Linnaeus and the Linnaeneans. Regnum Veg. 79:1-386.

Storey, W.B. (1958). Modification of sex expression in papaya. Hort. Adv., 2: 49-60.

Surguladze, Sh. M. (1979). Systematics and classification of the citrus fruits 15 Region- nauch- sessiya- soveta-botan-sadov- Zakavkaz ya- po- introduktsii- 1- akklimatiz- subtrop- rast- Tez- dokl, 62-63.

Terpo, A: (1985). Studies on taxonomy and grouping of pyruis species. Feddes - Repertorium ,96 (1-2):73-87.

Trehane, P., Brickell, C.D., Barum, B.R., Hetterscheid, W.L. A., Leslie, A.C., Mc

Tuz, A.S. (1978). Morphological and biological features of pear varieties (Pyrus L.) in relation to their origin. Turdy-po, 62 (3): 43-51.

Vavilov, N.I. (1951). Origin, variation, immunity and breedings of cultivated plants. Chron. Bot., 1: (6): 364.

Wang, H.K., Ding Y.X. and Yang, S.J. (1983). Muli-citron-a new variety of citrus grandis L. Acta Horticulturae Sinica, 10 (3) : 181-182.

WCMC (1992). Global Biodiversity : States of the Earth's living resources, Chapman and Hill, London.

Wiersema, J.H. and Leon, B. (1999). World economic plants : A standard references. CRC Press, Boca Raton, FL.

Wijanands, D.O. (1984). Nomenclature notes on the calamondin. Baileya, 22 (3) : 134-136.

Yadav, I.S. and Rajan, S. (1993). Genetic Resources of Mangifera. In: Advances in Horticulture, Vol. 1(Eds. K.L. Chadha and O.P. Pareek). Malhotra Publishing Hous, New Delhi, pp 77-93.

Important Definitions

Acuminate apex – When apex tapering gradually into a sharp point. (*Ficius religiosa*).

Acute – Leaf apex tapering to a sharp point but not stiff.

Adnate- When filament extends up to the whole length of anther.

Aggregate fruits- Such type of fruit develop from cluster of enlarged pistils of the same flower crowned into a mass e.g. blackberry, raspberry.

Alternate leaf – Arising of one leaf from each node.

Androecium – It is male reproductive whorl of flower, composed of stamens.

Anthophore – The internode between corolla and androecium is known as anthophore.

Axile placentation- In some compound pistils, the ovules are borne on the central axis e.g. *Citrus.*

Basifixed – Anther attached to the terminal of the filament.

Berry- The fruit develop from either monocarpellary or polycarpellary, syncarpous, ovary superior or inferior, in this case pericarp cannot be easily distinguished from mesocarp and endocarp.

Catkin – It is unisexual scaly spike which falls off in one piece.

Chemotaxonomy or Biochemical systematics- Classification of plants on the basis of chemical components present in plant body also known as biochemical systematics.

Cirrhose – When the leaf apex converts into coiling just tendril ending into thread like appendages e.g Banana.

Compound leaf – In compound leaf the margin incision reach upto midrib and break into number of leaflets, each leaf lets are devoid of axil buds.

Corymb – It is a similar to raceme, the lower flowers have longer stalks than the upper ones so that the inflorescence is some – what flat top.

Cultivar - A systematic group of cultivated plants that is clearly distinct, uniform and stable in its characteristics and which when propagated by asexual means retain these characteristics.

Cuspidate apex:- When a leaf converts into a sharp-pointed tip which is usually rigid e.g. date palm and pineapple.

Decidous Leaf – The leaves which die and fall off soon after end of the growing season.

Diadelphous - When stamens are connate in two groups.

Dorsifixed – In this case, filament appears to be affixed to the anther side eg. Passion flower.

Drupe- It is also called stone fruits, it develop from monocarpellary or polycarpellary, syncarpous superior ovary. It is always single seeded, epicarp, mesocarp and endocarp can be distinguished easily.

Elliptical – Ovate leaf blade with broadened in the middle of two end.

Epigynous – The receptable completely enclosed the ovary inside and floral parts grows above the ovary.

Epipetalous- Stamens borne on or apparently arising

from the corolla or petals.

Epiphyllus- When stamens arising from the perianth lobes e.g. Liliaceae family.

Epithet - A complete species name consists of the name of the genus to which the species belongs, plus the specific epithet and the author of the species.

Etaerio- An aggregate of simple fruits borne by single flower having apocarpous pistil, the ovaries of respective carpel mature into fruitlets clustered together on the pedicel. e.g. etaerio of berries (*Annona squamosa*). Drups (*Rubus idaeus*).

False fruit- A fruit in which thalamous or even the calyx is included along with the ovary as edible part e.g. apple, pear etc.

Flavedo- The outer yellow coloured portion of citrus fruit peel in which oil gland is embedded.

Foliaceous stipules- A large paired leafy outgrowth as seen in *Passiflora*.

Fruit - Botanically fruit is a repened ovary with or without other floral parts contributing in fruit development.

Fruit cycle- The time span between fruit set and maturity.

Fugacious Leaf - The leaves which fall off almost soon after their emergence.

Glabrous - Stem surface without any vestiture smooth but dull.

Glaucous - Stem surface without any vestiture, smooth and shining.

Glutinous surface - When the surface is covered with sticky, glutin like substance.

Gynandrophore - The condition of anthophore and

gynophore occurring in single flower is known as gynandrophore or gynandropsis.

Gynandrous- In this case, stamens adanate to or borne on the pistil.

Gynophore - The axis between the androecium and gynoecium is also elongated, called gynophore.

Heavy climber- The climbers with vigorous growth which require strong support like bower. E.g. *Passiflora edulis.*

Hillium- The point of attachment of the seed to its stalk.

Hispid hairs- Leaves are with rigid or bristly hairs.

Hypanthodium - It is special type of inflorescence in this case receptacle becomes fleshly and hollow with an interior opening guarded by hairy outgrowth, minute flowers are borne inside the cavity, the opening is known as ostiole. Pistils develop towards the base of the cavity and staminate flowers towards the upper regions (near ostiole) eg *Ficus.*

Hypogynous receptacle - In this case, thalamus is convex and floral parts took their position above this, it is called superior ovary.

Inflorescence - It is arrangement of the flower on the floral axis.

Lanceolate - The leaf is broadened at the base and tapering towards at the apex.

Mealy surface - Leaf surface covered with very minute, fine hairs, which can be rubbed - off easily like some powder.

Monoadelphous stamens- In this case, anther remain free, but stamens attached with their filament e.g. Malvaceae, family.

Multiple fruits- A fruit develop from an inflorescence where the flowers are crowded together and often fused one another forming a fruit e.g. pineapple, jackfruit etc.

Nut- Single seeded developing from a superior two or more syncarpous, carpel, pistil the pericarp convert into hard and woody shell.

Oblong - Leaf blades are wide and long with sides parallel or nearly parallel.

Obtuse - When the leaf apex is rounded.

Opposite leaf - Two leaves arising from a node one on the opposite side of the twig from the others.

Oval - Leaf blade broadly elliptical with the breadth considerably more than half of the length.

Ovary- The pistil consists of an enlarged basal portion called the ovary, the ovary comprise one or more cavities (locules) within which small or egg- shaped ovules. The ovule attached the ovary wall by a small stalk called the funicle.

Ovate - Leaf blade like egg shaped slightly broader at the base and tapering at apex.

Pale chemotaxonomy- It is a system of classification in which biochemical presence are utilized from fossil plants for comprehend and accurate classification.

Pariental placentation- In the compound ovary has a single locules but as many placenta as there are carpels. The placentae are on the inner side of the ovary wall. The number of placenta indicate number of carpel.

Perigynous - In this case, the receptable form cup shaped structure and floral parts found around this eg stone fruits.

Peristent Leaf - The leaves which continue to survive and functional for one or more years.

Phylloclade - It is modification of stem, more or less flattened functioning like a leaf.

Pistil- It is also known as gynoecium consist stigma, style and ovary.

Placenta- The intrusion of the ovary wall into the locule to which the ovules remain attached is called placenta. Further, the mode of arrangement of the ovules within an ovary is called placentation.

Poly adelphous stamens- When filaments are arranged into two groups e.g. lemon.

Pome- These are the fruit developing from the polycarpellary, syncarpous, inferior ovary. It is large made up of the fleshy receptacle, the ovary forming the core as in apple and pear.

Prickle – It is also a type of spine grows on the bark or epidermis of stem e.g. as found in Roses.

Priority - It is a principle of ICBN stating that the earliest published name is the proper name assigned to a species.

Pubescent – Surface covered with dense or sparse hairy outgrowth, but soft, short and straight hairs.

Racemose Inflorescence – The inflorescence axis does not terminate into a flower but continue to grow indefinitely and bears flower laterally in acropetal fashion. The older flower have long pedicels.

Simple fruit- It develop from solitary pistil consist of one enlarge ovary with which other flower parts may be incorporated.

Simple leaf – Each leaf have bud in axil.

Simple pistil- It consist one carpel with one or more ovule may produced.

Spadix – It is a type of spike enclosed by a large modified leaf known as spathe.

Spike – It is racemose inflorescence flowers are sessile.

Stem – It is ascending portion of the plant, develop from plumule as provide the support for leaves, flowers and fruits.

Stipules – It is lateral appendages arising at the base of the leaf, it protect the leaves in the bud state. If leaves are present with stipules are known as stipulate, when abscent exstipulate.

Synandrous stamens- When stamens are connate throughout their length by both filament and anthers.

Syncarpous- A pistil contain more than one carpel, united (syncarpous) or free (apocarpous) carpels with their enclosed ovules.

Syngenesious stamens- In this condition, stamens are connate by their anther and filaments remain free.

Taxometrics (Numerical taxonomy) - it is model aspect of taxonomy in which high magnificence electron microscopes cum computers are used in taxonomy for a quantitative data collection which form basis for classification.

Tendril – It is generally modification of the stem into rotating or twisting thread like extension by which a plant grasp an object and climb to it.

Thallamus – It is condensed, swollen end of flower axis, which supports the floral appendages. In majority of flowers the receptable is extremely reduced structure, but in certain cases, become elongated and exhibits distinct nodes and internodes.

Thorn – Strong, sharp, pointed woody body mostly, arising from the wood.

Tomentose – It is wooly matted hairs curled and appressed to the surface covered.

Umbel – The flowers are pedicellate, pedicels seems to be arise from single point.

Versatile - Filament attached to a point of the anther and appears it swing freely.

Brief Systematics of Minor Fruits

S. No.	Common Name	Scientific Name	Order	Family
1	Jamun	*Syzygium cuminii* Skeel.	Myrtales	Myrtaceae
2	tamarind	*Tamarindus indica* L.	Leguminales	Leguminoceae
3	Lasoda	*Cordia myxa* Roxb	Polymoniales	
4	Karonda	*Carissa carandas* L.	Apocynales	Apocynaceaes
5	Bael	*Aegle marmelos* Corr	Rutales	Rutaceae
6	Pilu	*Salvadora oleoides* decae	Celastrales	salvadoraceae
7	Mangosteen	*Garcinia mangostena* L.	Guttiferales	Guttiferae
8	Sapota	*Manilkara achras* Fosberg	Ebenales	Sapotaceae
9	Loquat	*Eriobotrya japonica* Lindl	Rosales	Rosaceae
10	Woodapple	*Feronia limonia* L.	Geranials	Rutaceae
11	Aonla	*Emblica officinalis* Gaerth	Euphorbiales	Euphorbiaceae
12	Charoli	*Buchanania lazan* Spreng	Sapindales	Anacardiaceae
13	Khirni	*Manilkara hexandra*	Ebenales	Sapotaceae
14	Kokum	*Garcinia indica*	Parietales	Guttiferae
15	Marking nut	*Semicarpus anacardium*	Sapindales	Anacardiaceae
16	Phalsa	*Grewia asiatica* L.	Tiliales	Tiliaceae
17	Drumstick	*Moringa pterigosperma*	Rhoeadales	Moringaceae
18	Paniala	*Flacourtia jangomas*	Bixales	Flacourtiaceae
19	Kamrakh	*Averrhoa carambola*	Geraniales	Oxalidaceae
20	Durian	*Durio zebathinus*	Malvales	Malvaceae
21	Passion fruit	*Passiflora edulis*	Passiflorales	Passifloraceae
22	Barbados Cherry	*Malpighia punicifolia*	Geraniales	Malpighiaceae
23	Chalta/ elephant apple	*Dellenia indica*	Delleniales	Dilleniaceae

Index

Vicar of Wink Field in Full bearing fruits are abnormally big size

Trifocitrus (*Poncirus trifoliata*) fruits in bearing, Used as cold hardy root stocks

Wild peach fruits used for raising seedlings

Poncirus trifoliate fruits , seed are bold

Seeds of Trifocitrus

Golden Delicious Apple

Crab Apple

Red Gold Apple cultivars

Apple cultivar Lal Ambri

Crab Apple fruit

Apple cultivar Lal Ambri

Tral apple

Ambri Apple indigenous to Kashmir

Grafted walnut Trees
in bearing after five years

Red Gold Apple cultivars mainly used as pollinizers

Walnut trees bears fruit on terminal

Vicar of Wink Field fruit of pear

Prunus salicina (Japanese plum) have large number of spurs

Pecan nut bears in cluster 2 to 5 terminally

Kiwifruit cv. Hayward

Kiwifruit 15 Years old in Full Bearing, single Vine yield 60- 70 Kgs

Peach cultivars South land

Peach cultivars South land

Apricot cultivars Harcot

Apricot cultivars Harcot

Apricot cv. Orgrand

Orgrand Apricot variety

Ambri apple: indigenous to Kashmir

Tree of Wild apple : *Malus baccata*

Fruiting spur of cherry

Walnut terminal shoot

Red Gold apple cultivars : a good pollinizers and heavy bearer

Pear : Willium Bartlette cultivars

Wild Pear in bearing

Nut covered in the hulls

Hazelnut : Nut in the green spiny hull

Hazelnut catkin

Nuts of the Hazelnut